SCHOLASTIC

Scottish Primary Year 3

50 Shared texts

NON-FICTION

INCLUDES CD-ROM

Sue Taylor

Credits

Author
Sue Taylor

Series Consultants
Huw Thomas
Melissa Mackinlay

Project Manager
Elizabeth Dalby

Editor
Roanne Charles

Assistant Editor
Rachel Mackinnon

Series Designer
Anna Oliwa

Designers
Lynne Joesbury
Helen Taylor
Micky Pledge

Text © 2007 Sue Taylor
© 2007 Scholastic Ltd

Designed using Adobe InDesign

Published by Scholastic Ltd
Villiers House
Clarendon Avenue
Leamington Spa
Warwickshire CV32 5PR

www.scholastic.co.uk

Printed by Bell and Bain Ltd, Glasgow

1 2 3 4 5 6 7 8 9   7 8 9 0 1 2 3 4 5 6

British Library Cataloguing-in-Publication Data
A catalogue record for this book is available from the British Library.

ISBN 0-439-96565-9
ISBN 978-0439-96565-1

Due to the nature of the web, we cannot guarantee any of the content or links of any sites featured. We strongly recommend that teachers check websites before using them in the classroom.

System requirements
- Supported PC operating systems: Windows 98 SE, Windows ME, Windows 2000, Windows NT, Windows XP
- Supported Mac operating systems: Mac OS9 with CarbonLib 1.6[1], Mac OSX
- Recommended minimum processor speed: 1GHz
- Recommended minimum RAM: 512MB

Mac OSX version 10.1 and Intel-based Macs
If you are experiencing problems, please double click the icon named "os9 autorun" on the CD-ROM. This will run the Mac OS9 version of the program.

[1]Some versions of Mac OS9 do not have CarbonLib 1.6 installed. Please visit the Apple website (www.apple.com) to download and install CarbonLib 1.6.

Contents

 Teachers' notes    Photocopiable

N *Teacher's notes*   P *Photocopiable*

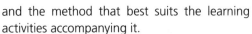

Introduction

The new *50 Shared Texts Non-fiction* series follows Scholastic's previously published series, *50 Shared Texts*. It picks up on two comments received from a number of teachers in response to the initial series. Firstly they welcomed the notes that accompanied each text, providing various avenues for discussion with a class as part of the shared or guided reading of the text. Secondly, they wanted more non-fiction. By 'more' they meant both 'more texts' in general, and texts from a wider range of backgrounds.

This new series aims to meet those needs, by building on the most valuable aspects of the original series. The provision of a range of high-quality extracts gives you the time to focus on teaching rather than sourcing material; relevant links with other areas of the curriculum are highlighted; and the book can be easily used in a flexible way and dipped into as required.

Shared reading
Shared reading has been around as a specific term since the work of Don Holdaway in New Zealand. The idea gained momentum during the 1980s but the main push for both 'shared' and 'guided' approaches to reading took off with the arrival of the National Literacy Strategy, introduced by the Government to schools in England and Wales in 1997. The approaches have also found a home in classrooms in Scotland and further afield.

Shared reading is the strategy in which the teacher reads a text with the whole class. This can be everyone reading along together or the teacher giving instructions such as 'read the first paragraph in your head'. It can include the teacher reading and pointing to the words while the children observe, or the teacher asking a child to read a portion of the text aloud. The key ingredient is everyone having sight of the same text and taking their eyes along the same lines at the same time.

This series incorporates a range of approaches to shared reading, dependent on the age of the children, the best approach to the specific text

and the method that best suits the learning activities accompanying it.

While the series is entitled 50 Shared Texts it also allows for the fact that some teachers may want to use certain texts in the context of guided reading. Guided reading involves a teacher or teaching assistant working with a small group of children to guide them through a text, setting them off on their reading to a particular point, stopping them along the way and asking questions or discussing observations. The texts and notes in this resource can be used in this context.

What's in the book
The texts in this book are organised term by term, and cover a range of examples of non-fiction tailored to each year group. Each text appears in two forms. The small, annotated version and accompanying page of teachers' notes guide you through features in the text that lend themselves to learning objectives. The larger, un-annotated version is to use with your class and can be copied or enlarged.

What's on the CD-ROM
All 50 texts from the book also feature on the CD-ROM, in a variety of full-colour formats designed to maximise their potential for sharing with a group.

The CD-ROM contains:
● Colour versions of all 50 core texts.
● Fully annotated versions of the 50 core texts.
● Half-annotated versions of the 50 core texts, designed for use with interactive whiteboard tools – providing you with the opportunity to highlight, circle and underline key words and phrases.
● The 50 core texts in an editable format, allowing you or the children to make changes to the document and print out the results.
● Differentiated full-colour versions of all 50 texts. These are designed to support less able learners, though most can also be used with the whole class: to teach the structure of the various non-fiction genres, to scaffold writing tasks, or alongside the core text as a comparison between written and visual methods of presenting information.
● Print options for all the text versions.

The texts

The 50 core texts featured in the book and on the CD-ROM have been either gathered from a range of diverse backgrounds or specially written for this resource to fit with the objectives for each term. The crucial aim of this gathering is that it should save you time, providing you with a ready-to-use range of stimulating and appropriate magazine articles, website extracts, newspaper cuttings, reference material, advertisements, posters and leaflets to explore, rather than expecting you to spend time hunting them down yourself. For most text types, there is more than one example, allowing you to select the one that best supports your planning requirements.

The purpose-written texts have been devised to provide texts that dovetail with the objectives being explored in a particular unit of learning. The authors have aimed to cover a range of learning objectives, making full use of the texts to support text level objectives while also ensuring there is coverage at sentence and word level.

Background

Notes are provided about the text that may include details about its origin or author, the story behind it or the context in which it was printed. This section can also include notes from the author about the rationale for using a particular text in the way it is dealt with in this resource.

Discussing the text

Guidance is provided as to how each text can be explored in the classroom setting. The aim is to avoid bland

questions and answers and to provide ways of engaging children in reading and interpreting the text. This can include discussion points, activities they may undertake that weave their way through a reading of the text, points of contention where they may disagree with it and language features that will lead them to further explore their own grasp of words.

Some of these sections contain a lot of material and it is up to you to be selective. The aim in each section is to provide more material than needed.

The texts

The choice of texts has been driven by the need to ensure that these are quality texts both in content and language. It is hoped that among the selection you will find a mixture of authors and texts, both familiar and new. Whole texts have been provided as far as possible so that children have the satisfaction of reading and appreciating a coherent and complete piece of writing.

Talk, read and write

This section leads on from the reading to provide activities stemming from the text. Following a discussion of the text, this section provides activities that link with the reading. These may lend themselves to independent or group work within literacy lessons or they could be activities that will fit in with other areas of the curriculum.

Extension

This section provides ideas for further exploration of themes covered in the text, and relevant homework activities suitable for the year group.

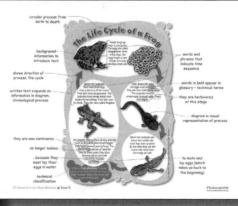

Range and objectives

Year 2 Term 1

Range	Text	NLS references
Recounts (revision from Year 1)	**'How we made a puppet whale'** by Sue Taylor	(Y1: 3: T18), (Y1: 3: T20), S2, S3
Instructional texts	**'Puppets'** from *Arts and Crafts Around the World*	W3, W10, T13, T14
	'Easy pop-ups – hippo ballerina' from *The Usbourne Book of Pop-ups* by Richard Dungworth and Ray Gibson	W10, S5, T13, T14
	'Swedish hanging biscuits' from *You and Your Child: Christmas* by Ray Gibson	W3, W4, W10, T13, T14
	'How to make wholemeal bread rolls' by Sue Taylor	W10, S5, T13, T14, T17
	'Route map' from *Discovery World Stage F: Maps*	W10, S5, S6, T15, T17
	'Snakes and Ladders' by Sue Taylor	S2, T3, T13, T14, T15, T16
	'How to play hopscotch' by Sue Taylor	W9, S2, T13, T14, T15, T16, T17
	'String games – cup and saucer' by Sue Taylor	S4, T13, T15, T18
	'Mixing colours to paint a rainbow' by Sue Taylor	W9, W10, S6, T13, T14
	'Painting butterflies' by Sue Taylor	W7, S2, T13, T14
	'How to look after a hamster' by Sue Taylor	W10, S4, T13, T14, T15, T17, T18
	'Making sentences with Roamer' by Valiant Technology	W10, S5, S6, T13, T15, T18
	'Classroom rules' by Sue Taylor	W9, S4, T13, T15, T18
	'How to "grow" a Japanese Wishing Tree' by Sue Taylor	W1, S2, S4, S5, T13, T14
	'Be safe with fireworks!' by Sue Taylor	W9, S3, S4, T13, T17, T18
	'Making dummy fireworks 1' from *Bright Ideas: Festivals* by Jill Bennett and Archie Millar	W10, S4, T15, T16, T17, T18

Year 2 Term 2

Range	Text	NLS references
Dictionaries	**'Dictionary extract: whale–which'** from *Collins Junior Dictionary*	W3, W4, S7, T16, T17
	'Science dictionary: ad–bl' from *Science Dictionary*	W5, S7, T17, T20
	'Maths dictionary: -teen' by Scholastic Ltd	S7, T17, T18, T20
	'Rhyming dictionary: shore' from *Oxford Rhyming Dictionary* by John Foster	W2, S7, T16, T18
Alphabetically ordered texts – thesauruses	**'Thesaurus – bad and good'** from *Oxford First Thesaurus* by Andrew Delahunty	W8, W10, W11, S9, T18
Other alphabetically ordered texts	**'Class 2 directory'** by Sue Taylor	W6, S7, S8, T18
	'Class 2 library catalogue' by Sue Taylor	W2, W3, W5, S7, T18
Indexes	**'Catalogue index'** by Scholastic Ltd	W4, W5, S7, S8, T18
Glossaries and indexes	**'Glossary and index'** by Sue Taylor	W5, S9, T16, T17, T18, T20
Explanations	**'The life cycle of a frog'** by Sue Taylor	W3, S9, T19, T21
	'Which comes first – the chicken or the egg?' by Sue Taylor	S9, T19, T20, T21
	'How does you garden grow? The life of a bean' by Sue Taylor	W1, W10, T19, T20, T21
	'Where does bread come from?' by Sue Taylor	W3, W5, S8, T19, T20, T21
	'The journey of a letter' by Sue Taylor	W9, T19, T20, T21
	'Touch' from *Usbourne Flip-Flaps: How do your senses work?* by Judy Tatchell and Alastair Smith	W10, W11, S7, T19, T20, T21
	'Change – ice, water, steam' by Sue Taylor	W11, T19, T20, T21
	'Shuttle mission' from *My Best Book of Spaceships* by Ian Graham	W5, S5, S9, T19, T20

Year 2 Term 3

Range	Text	NLS references
Information books	**'A bakery burns down'** from *Beginning History: Plague and Fire* by Rhoda Nottridge and **'Fire!'** from *Our World: Tudor and Stuart Times* by Jane Shuter, Adam Hook and Judith Maguire	S3, S6, T13, T14, T16
	'Extracts from the diary of Samuel Pepys' from *Our World: Tudor and Stuart Times* by Jane Shuter, Adam Hook and Judith Maguire	S6, T13, T14, T16
	'Book blurb – elephants' from *Natural World – Elephant* by Will Travers	S6, T5, T13, T18
	'Meet the elephant' from *Natural World – Elephant* by Will Travers	W9, T16, T18, T19
Information books including non-chronological reports	**'Reptiles of long ago'** by Scholastic Ltd	W2, T13, T14, T16, T17, T19
Information books	**'Solar System – contents and index'** from *Usbourne Beginners: Sun, Moon and Stars* by Stephanie Turnbull	W9, T13, T15, T17, T18
Information books including non-chronological reports	**'What is the sun?'** from *Sun and Us* by Jillian Powell	W3, T14, T16, T18, T19, T20, T21
	'Magnets' by Sue Taylor	W9, T16, T17, T18
	'The Smith family in 2005' by Scholastic Ltd	T13, T19, T20, T21
	'The Watson family in 1905' by Scholastic Ltd	W9, T13, T14, T19, T20, T21
	'The seaside' from *Step by Step Geography: Seas and Coasts* by Patience Coster	W9, T14, T19, T20, T21
	'Contents pages' by Scholastic Ltd	W9, T14, T15, T17, T18
Information books	**'Email addresses'** from *The Usbourne Guide to e-mail* by Mark Wallace and Philippa Wingate	W9, T16, T19, T20
Information books including non-chronological reports	**'Spiders'** from Literacy World: Stage 4: *Spiders and how they hunt* by Jason Amber	W9, S4, S6, T14, T17, T20
	'Healthy food' from *Food and your health* by Jillian Powell	W2, W9, S4, T13
	'Rainforests' from *Questions and Answers – Rainforest Animals* by Michael Chinery	T16, T17, T20

Puppet whale

by Sue Taylor

Background

This text tells of a group's simple puppet-making activity. It revises features of recounts and links to the next text – instructions for the same activity. The text includes a chronological ordering of events, with time connectives, and uses the first person and past tense. In conjunction with the next extract, it can be used to highlight language styles used for different types of writing that serve different purposes. The context relates to science, and design and technology topics, particularly movement and mechanisms.

What's on the CD-ROM

This version adapts the core text as a writing frame. It retains the illustrations and uses sentence starters as a means of supporting children's writing. In most cases, these are the time connectives, which draw attention to the way in which these words link the events in the core text. The frame can be used in guided writing, using the pictures as a prompt for sequencing. Children can generate simple sentences to describe each stage of the process, rehearsing sentences orally before writing.

Discussing the text

● Before looking at this text, the children should make the puppets. Use the instructions in the following text, if appropriate. After making the puppets, generate a class set of notes as a reminder of what was done.

● Now introduce the text, saying that it is your recount of the activity. Remind the children about work on recounts in Year 1, noting that they are used to retell events that have happened (in the past) and they describe events and actions in the order in which they happened (chronological order).

● Read the title and draw attention to the bold type. Note the use of *we*, because the text describes what you and the class did, and the past tense *made*, because it was something done earlier.

● Read the recount and ask the children to discuss in pairs whether it describes what they did accurately. Is there anything they want to add to or change in the recount?

● Now consider the pictures, discussing how they help the reader understand the process.

● Highlight *we* in each sentence. Then, in a different colour, highlight the past tense verbs. Notice how they are used consistently throughout the text.

● Focus on the last sentence and ask the children how it is different from the rest of the text. Note the use of *you* instead of *we* and present tense rather than past. Draw out understanding that this is a closing sentence that is no longer talking about the process of making the puppets; it is a description of what the puppet can do now it has been made.

● Highlight the time connectives *First* and *Then* at the beginning of the first two sentences. Discuss how words like these help to show the order in which things happened and how they link one sentence with the next. Ask children to come out and highlight other connectives.

● Confirm the order of tasks. Could any have been done in a different order? Steps 2 and 3 could be reversed without significant effect, but the phrase *on another part of the card* indicates a sequence.

● Circle the comma after each connective and model how to read the sentence with the right expression, emphasising the connective and separating it from the rest of the sentence with a pause. Discuss the commas in the two sentences without time connectives, used to separate extra information from the main sentence.

Talk, read and write

● Give the children cut-up versions of the text, and ask them to match the text to the pictures and then sequence events correctly.

● Use cloze versions of the text, without connectives, to focus on the importance of connectives in linking sentences.

● In guided writing, help the children to compose a recount of another event they have all shared, using the key genre features. It could be a classroom routine such as going to lunch, which might lead to a poster of instructions.

Extension

Children could draw a sequence of pictures to recount something they have done at home, labelling the pictures with connectives. Some children could write a sentence for each.

1: 3: T20: to write simple recounts

list of equipment and materials needed before starting

past tense verbs describing what they did

diagrams aid understanding

2: 1: S3: to recognise and take account of commas in reading aloud with appropriate expression

present tense verbs describe what puppet does when it has been finished

How we made a puppet whale

First, we got some card, a pencil, a pair of scissors, a paper fastener, some sticky tape and two sticks.

Then, we drew the body and tail of a whale on the card.

Next, we drew it's mouth on another part of the card.

After that, we cut out the two parts.

To make the mouth move, we joined the body and the mouth with a paper fastener.

Finally, we stuck one stick on the body and one stick on the mouth with sticky tape.

When you move the sticks, the whale's mouth opens and shuts.

Text © 2007, Sue Taylor; notebook clip art © Nova Developments

first person plural – group of participants, personal recount

past tense – telling about something that has happened

time connectives at start of sentences indicate sequence clearly; steps/ events in chronological order

comma separates connective or clause from rest of sentence; help reader to pause and use correct expression

not we, because no longer about process that was followed but general statement involving general participants

1: 3: T18: to read recounts and begin to recognise generic structure

2: 1: S2: to find examples of words and phrases that link sentences

Puppets

from Arts and Crafts Around the World

Background

These instructions can be linked to the previous text to compare the structural and language features of each text type and see how each meets the needs of its audience. This text has typical features of instructions, including a list of materials and equipment, numbered steps and imperative verbs. It also includes illustrations to help understanding. The activity can link to science, design and technology, and art and design. Puppets could be used to develop drama and storytelling techniques, and adapted to link with other topics such as history or RE.

What's on the CD-ROM

This simplified version of the core text has a labelled diagram to support each stage. This visual material will help less able readers to engage with the text. This text can be used in guided reading to explore sequencing and the use of imperatives.

Discussing the text

● If being used in conjunction with the previous text, recap the puppet-making activity and the recount. Explain to the children that they are now going to look at a text that will tell someone else how to make a puppet. If being used in isolation, use the instructions as a starting point for puppet-making, and, if possible, display a range of puppets.

● Begin reading, and ask the children to consider the purpose of the picture and the first paragraph. This paragraph is not part of the instructions; it gives background information about puppets. Encourage children to share their experiences of puppets or puppet shows.

● Explain *3D*, making links to shape in maths. If possible demonstrate how different puppets are *3D images*.

● Read the next sentence, which is the beginning of the actual instructions, and the list of materials and equipment needed. Consider why this list needs to be at the beginning.

● Read the instructions, referring to the pictures to aid understanding. Ask why each instruction has a number. Try re-ordering them and see how this affects the overall sense. Note the words in each step that link back to a previous one (*the animal* in step 2 refers to a *simple animal shape* drawn in step 1).

● Highlight the first word of each instruction (the imperative) and ask the children what these have in common. Help the children to understand these as the 'bossy' words, using the terms *verb* and *imperative* if appropriate. Illustrate by giving the children simple instructions to carry out, such as **Clap** *your hands.*

● Note that step 4 actually contains two instructions, linked by *and*, and therefore has two imperatives. Reinforce this by asking pairs to give each other two instructions linked by *and,* such as **Stand** up and **clap** your hands.

● For a word-level focus, highlight the 'ow' phoneme in *how* and *out,* noting the different spellings of the same sound. Ask the children to generate (in pairs on individual whiteboards) other words with the 'ow' phoneme and to classify them into two spelling groups.

● Repeat this with the 'ar' phoneme in *card* and *part*, and, depending on the accent common in the class, compare with the spelling of *fast(ener).*

Talk, read and write

● If not already done, organise groups to make puppets, following and evaluating the instructions. Ask the children to suggest changes or additions to the text or pictures.

● Use the puppets for storytelling, with groups performing short plays based on the animals or characters they have made. These dramas could be linked to a topic in another curriculum area.

● If the previous text (recount) was used, compare the two texts in guided reading sessions. Look closely at the structure and language features of each text, compiling a comparison chart. Discuss when each text might be used, by whom and for what purpose.

● Develop the word-level learning by asking the children to find other examples of the 'ow' and/or 'ar' phonemes in their reading books, and to sort them into spelling patterns.

Extension

Ask children to find a set of instructions at home and to identify the imperatives. They could also look for words with the 'ow' and/or 'ar' phonemes.

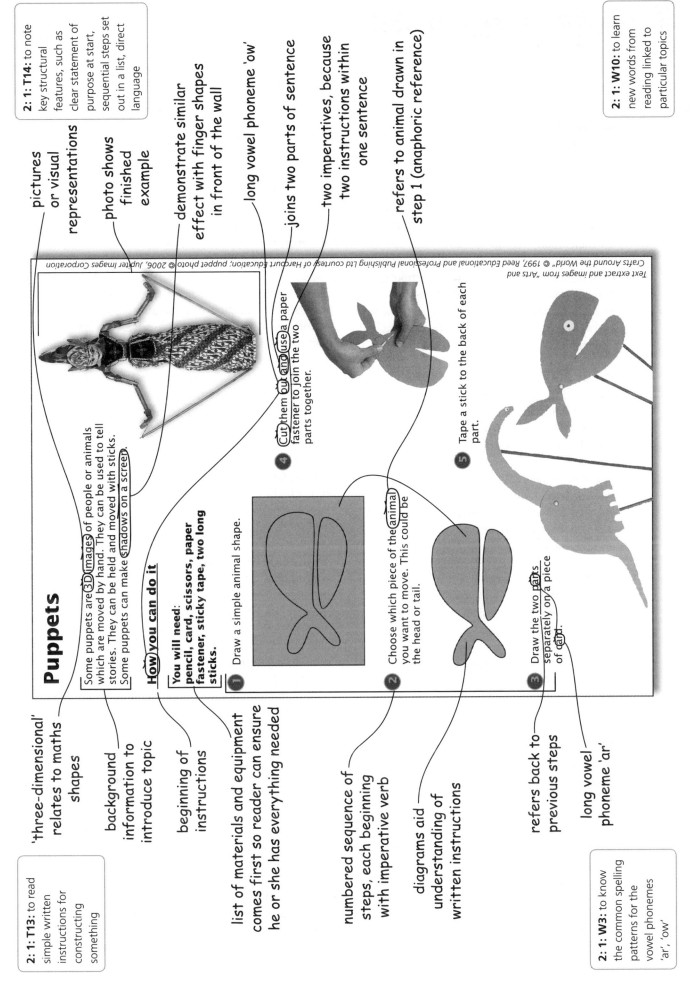

Puppets

Some puppets are 3D images of people or animals which are moved by hand. They can be used to tell stories. They can be held and moved with sticks. Some puppets can make shadows on a screen.

How you can do it

You will need: pencil, card, scissors, paper fastener, sticky tape, two long sticks.

1. Draw a simple animal shape.
2. Choose which piece of the animal you want to move. This could be the head or tail.
3. Draw the two parts separately on a piece of card.
4. Cut them out and use a paper fastener to join the two parts together.
5. Tape a stick to the back of each part.

Text extract and images from "Arts and Crafts Around the World" © 1997, Reed Educational and Professional Publishing Ltd courtesy of Harcourt Education; puppet photo © 2006, Jupiter Images Corporation

---

2: 1: T14: to note key structural features, such as clear statement of purpose at start, sequential steps set out in a list, direct language

2: 1: W10: to learn new words from reading linked to particular topics

2: 1: T13: to read simple written instructions for constructing something

2: 1: W3: to know the common spelling patterns for the vowel phonemes 'ar', 'ow'

Annotations:
- pictures or visual representations
- photo shows finished example
- demonstrate similar effect with finger shapes in front of the wall
- long vowel phoneme 'ow'
- joins two parts of sentence
- two imperatives, because two instructions within one sentence
- refers to animal drawn in step 1 (anaphoric reference)
- 'three-dimensional' relates to maths shapes
- background information to introduce topic
- beginning of instructions
- list of materials and equipment comes first so reader can ensure he or she has everything needed
- numbered sequence of steps, each beginning with imperative verb
- diagrams aid understanding of written instructions
- refers back to previous steps
- long vowel phoneme 'ar'

Easy pop-ups

by Richard Dungworth and Ray Gibson

Background

Pop-up cards are popular with most children and some may have bought, or even made, such cards for friends and family. This text gives instructions for making an amusing pop-up card that can be adapted to children's individual interests and tastes by selecting a different character and pop-up element. The written procedure is accompanied by illustrations and demonstrates many key features of instructional texts, such as the list of materials needed, and sequenced, numbered steps using imperative verbs. There are clear cross-curricular links to design and technology.

What's on the CD-ROM

This set of instructions is for a simpler pop-up card. In this case there are only four steps and the pictures are more crucial in supporting the text. This will enable less able readers to take part in the activity of constructing a card but with fewer reading demands. The text nevertheless demonstrates the same key features of instructional texts as the core text and can, therefore, be used in guided reading sessions for similar purposes.

Discussing the text

● Ensure you have an example of 'one you made earlier' and, if possible, other pop-ups.

● Read the title and subtitle, noting the initial capital letters. Take the opportunity for the children to share their knowledge and experience of pop-ups.

● Read the full text and ask what kind of text it is. What is its purpose? Who might use it? Elicit the word *instructions* – a text written to tell someone how to do something. Encourage the children to talk about their experiences of using instructions for different purposes.

● Re-read the text in sections and establish the purpose of each. Confirm any difficult vocabulary as it arises.

● Identify and label the title, subtitle, items needed (discuss measurements at an appropriate level) and numbered instructions.

● Look at other presentational features such as the use of bold and well-spaced paragraphs and consider why they are used. Elicit that the illustrations show the reader what the pop-up should look like.

● Re-order the sections (using whiteboard tools or on an enlarged paper copy) and ask the children what difference this makes.

● Go on to ask why the instructions are numbered. Could they be followed in any order? Why not? (Prompt the children to refer to details in the text in their responses.)

● Highlight the imperatives in the first instruction, one for each sentence. Ask the children what these words mean and how they work. Give a child a simple instruction to illustrate the function of imperatives, such as *Stand up; Walk to the door*. Go back to the text and ensure that the children have understood that these are the words that tell the reader what to do. Notice the direct language – 'talking' to the person carrying out the instructions – and their position at the beginning of the sentence.

● Now highlight the imperatives in step 2 (establishing meaning if necessary). Then ask the children in pairs to discuss and identify the rest of the imperatives. Ask individuals to highlight them on the board and draw attention again to their position in the sentence.

Talk, read and write

● Support small groups in following the instructions to make the cards. Ask them to evaluate the instructions and, if they think they are needed, to suggest improvements or alternatives, for example in the layout.

● Other groups can make posters to illustrate key features of instructional texts, using a large copy of the text for annotation. As they do this, ask them to look out for capital letters.

● Give mixed-ability pairs cut up copies of the text to reassemble in order.

● Make cloze copies of the text with the imperatives omitted and ask the children to fill in the gaps. (Give some children a bank of words to choose from.)

● Collect and classify imperative verbs for different types of instructions, to be added to as other texts are read.

Extension

Ask children to find examples of instructions in the classroom and at home for display. Ask them to take one set of instructions and identify the key features discussed.

Easy pop-ups

Hippo ballerina
This hippopotamus ballet dancer has a pop-up ballet skirt.

You will need:
a piece of pink paper 20 × 10cm (8 × 4in); a piece of thick, white paper 19 × 19cm (7½ × 7½in); a pencil; felt-tip pens; glue.

1. Lay the pink paper down with its long edges at the sides. Fold down a 2cm (¾in) strip at the top edge.

2. Turn the paper over and fold down another 2cm (¾in). Repeat this step until you run out of paper.

3. Put glue on one side of the strip. Fold it in half so that its ends meet. Press while the glue dries.

4. Fold the piece of white paper in half to make a card. Draw a hippo ballerina across the inside of the fold.

5. Glue the accordion strip onto your ballerina, so that its folded end is against the middle crease.

6. Put some glue on top of the strip and carefully close the card. Press down while the glue dries.

7. When you open the card, the pink accordion-folded strip will fan out like a ballet skirt.

Text extract and illustration from "The Usborne Book of Pop-ups" by Richard Dungworth and Ray Gibson; illustration by Teri Gower © 1995, Usborne Publishing Ltd

---

Annotations:

2: 1: T14: to note key structural features, such as clear statement of purpose at start, sequential steps set out in a list, direct language

picture shows goal – how finished card should look

some imperatives not at the beginning of the step; some not at the beginning of a sentence

not an instruction (no imperative) instead, describes how finished card should now work

2: 1: W10: to learn new words from reading linked to particular topics

2: 1: T13: to read simple written instructions for constructing something

main title – large, bold and brief to draw attention

subheading giving specific topic also in bold; also works as picture caption/title

brief description of item and its particular pop-up feature

list of items needed, separated by semicolons

measurements given in metric and imperial – important to stick to one

numbered sequence of imperative sentences

2: 1: S5: to revise knowledge about other uses of capitalisation, such as for headings, titles

Swedish hanging biscuits by Ray Gibson

Background

These biscuits are traditionally made in Sweden to hang on the Christmas tree. The recipe can be used in the classroom, and children will enjoy making the biscuits and then evaluating the instructions. The recipe could be adapted for another context. Typical of instructional texts it includes a list of materials and sequenced steps using imperatives. It also offers additional hints, and the written text is supported by illustrations. Crucially, the recipe does *not* state how many biscuits can be made. (About 24, depending on cutter size.) The text introduces a particular type of instructions and develops subject-specific vocabulary. There are links to science, and design and technology. It also provides a good context for understanding measures in maths.

What's on the CD-ROM

This is a simpler biscuit recipe. It contains fewer materials and steps, to enable less able readers to carry out the cooking activity. The steps are numbered for additional clarity and subject-specific vocabulary is retained. This text can be used in guided reading to explore key genre features, and recipes in particular, and therefore meet similar objectives.

Discussing the text

● Present the text and ask the children to consider what kind of text it is. Where it might be found and who might use it? How do we know it is a recipe? Share experiences of cooking at home or in school.

● Display ingredients and equipment to enable vocabulary to be understood before reading.

● Look at each section in turn, without yet reading the whole text, and work together to label these sections. Consider the purpose of each feature and its position on the page.

● Now read each section in detail, clarifying vocabulary and concepts that might be unfamiliar.

● Note that recipes are a very particular type of instructions and contain many words and ideas specific to cooking. Discuss weights and measures (metric and imperial), including oven temperatures, at an appropriate level.

● Consider how the pictures provide visual support for the written text, *showing* what might be difficult to explain or understand through words alone.

● Point out that the steps in the method are not numbered. How does the reader know in what order to follow them? Note the additional *Hint* giving advice to the reader.

● Highlight the imperatives in the first three instructions and elicit that these are the 'bossy' words that tell the reader what to do. Note the direct language that addresses the reader and the fact that these words are always first in each instruction (note in the first and third steps that there are two imperatives because there are two instructions within one step).

● Ask the children to work in pairs to identify the imperatives in the remaining instructions.

● Now highlight *flour* in the ingredients, checking that the children know what it is, and compare it with *flower*. The two words sound the same but are spelled differently. Focus on the 'ow' phoneme and ask for suggestions of other words with the same phoneme, classifying them into *ou* and *ow* spellings.

Talk, read and write

● Help the children to make and taste the biscuits. Then ask them to evaluate the instructions, suggesting any additions or changes that would make them easier to follow.

● The children can make posters, identifying key features of recipes. For guided reading, provide copies of other simple recipes and identify these elements.

● Begin a glossary of cookery terms, particularly the technical imperatives, such as *Cream*, *Sift* and *blend*.

● Set up a kitchen role-play area, with recipes, equipment and packaging. Children could play the role of a television chef.

● For word-level work, ask the children to find and classify words with the vowel phoneme 'ow'. They could also explore other common homophones, such as *to/two/too*, writing sentences to show the different meanings.

Extension

Ask children to bring in recipes from home for comparison. A display might be linked to work on healthy eating.

2: 1: W4: to investigate and classify words with the same sounds but different spellings

2: 1: W10: to learn new words from reading linked to particular topics

first instruction is put separate and larger, to ensure oven has time to heat up

different ways of showing temperature, depending on type of oven

advice to ensure this part of the recipe works

which ingredients are wet and which are dry?

sequence of steps to follow in order, but not numbered or bulleted

this could be rolled out again for further biscuits

depends on oven

Swedish hanging biscuits

You will need:
225g (8oz) plain flour
½ teaspoon bicarbonate of soda
icing sugar
pinch of ground cloves
¾ teaspoon ground ginger
¾ teaspoon cinnamon
115g (4oz) margarine
115g (4oz) dark brown sugar
1 egg white

2 large bowls
Christmas biscuit cutters
sieve
baking tray
clingfilm
rolling pin
fish slice
wooden spoon
fat straw
fine ribbon
cooling rack

Set oven to:
180°C, 350°F Gas Mark 4

Hint
Don't put the hole too near the top of the biscuit or it will break when you hang it up.

Cream the margarine and sugar well, then beat in the egg white.

Sift the dry ingredients together in another bowl.

Add a little at a time to the creamed mixture, and blend together well to make a dough.

Wrap the dough in clingfilm and chill it for 30 minutes in the refrigerator, or ten minutes in the freezer.

Roll the dough out on a clean, floured surface, until it is about 5mm (¼in) thick.

Press biscuit cutters firmly into the dough. Peel away the extra dough.

Lift the shapes onto an ungreased baking tray, using a fish slice.

Press the end of a straw into the top of each shape, to make a hole.

Bake in the oven for ten to twelve minutes. Take out and cool on a cooling rack.

Text extract and illustrations from "You and Your Child: Christmas" by Ray Gibson © 1991, Usborne Publishing Ltd

2: 1: T13: to read simple recipes

'ow' phoneme; compare with 'flower'

lists of ingredients and kitchen equipment/tools given in separate columns, one item under another

imperative verbs; vocabulary specific to cookery

two instructions, and so two imperatives, within one sentence

freezer is colder than refrigerator so less time is needed for same effect

negative prefix 'un' means 'not'

2: 1: W3: to know the common spelling patterns for the vowel phonemes 'ar', 'ow'

Wholemeal bread rolls

by Sue Taylor

Background

Bread-making is a fascinating, although quite complex and time-consuming, process. Children will be able to make the bread in small groups in the classroom and observe the changes that occur. This learning makes links to changing materials in the science curriculum and it can also be linked to work on healthy eating. The recipe demonstrates many key features of the instructional genre, providing lists of ingredients and equipment, and numbered steps using imperative verbs. The structure of the recipe could be explored with the whole class in shared reading, and guided reading could be used for a closer look at the language. Subject-specific vocabulary (including weights and measures) can be explored at an appropriate level during the practical activity.

What's on the CD-ROM

The same recipe is reduced to its essential elements here, with simpler sentence structures. Although the recipe is still quite long, the simplified language will make it accessible through guided reading. Information omitted can be explored orally.

Discussing the text

● Show the text to the children, read the title and ask what kind of text it is. Discuss where texts like this are found. Share children's experiences of using recipes, noting that they are a particular type of instructional text, and of making and eating bread specifically. What other kinds of bread do they know? Which do they prefer?

● Note how the picture reinforces the goal expressed in the title. Why is it important to know how many rolls the recipe makes?

● Consider the meaning of *Preparation time*, which is identified separately from *Cooking time*. Note that together these show the 'baker' how much time will be needed to complete the recipe. Children might think that *1½ hours* is a long time for 'preparation'. The instructions will reveal that much of this time is needed for the dough to rise.

● Read the *Ingredients* (food items) and *Equipment* (tools) sections, ideally showing the class the items as they occur. Consider the importance of listing these at the beginning.

● Draw attention to the subheading *Method* (the instructions), and the numbered list that shows the sequence of steps clearly.

● Read the first instruction, discussing the function of the first word. Reinforce the 'bossy' nature of the imperative by playing *Simon Says*. (Note that in everyday speech we usually modify the direct instruction by using, for example, 'please'.)

● Ask the children to highlight other imperatives in the recipe, noting that some steps contain more than one instruction and, therefore, more than one imperative. Note instructions where the imperative is not the first word. In these cases, show how a connecting word or phrase is used to suggest time relationships.

● Read the warning at the end and discuss the effect of the large, bold capitals and exclamation marks, that engage the reader's attention and add emphasise. Although this comes at the end, it is vital that the reader takes note of it.

Talk, read and write

● Help the children to make the rolls in small groups, discussing the subject-specific concepts and vocabulary in context and observing the changes that occur.

● Ask the children to evaluate the recipe and outcome, suggesting any changes or additions for the next reader.

● Organise groups to make a fully-illustrated version of the recipe for younger children, drawing a picture of each step. Use shared and guided writing to model the composition of labels and simple captions to accompany each picture.

● Give children enlarged copies of the text and ask them to label key features of recipes. These can be used as posters for reference when writing similar texts.

● Use a kitchen role-play area to practise using the language of cooking.

Extension

Children can investigate different varieties of bread, at home or at the supermarket, drawing and labelling them for display. Make links to healthy eating. Ask children to bring in recipes from home for display and analysis.

what to do

many imperatives

lots of little steps to follow

disappears into the water

yeast needs to be warm (not hot) to work

indicates time relationship between two clauses

extra advice

time connectives

oven temperatures vary a little

Text © 2007, Sue Taylor; photo © 2006, Jupiter Images Corporation

How to make wholemeal bread rolls

Method:

1 Wash your hands.

2 Put the warm water in a jug and stir in the sugar. Stir until the sugar dissolves. Add the yeast and mix well.

3 Leave the mixture in a warm place for about ten minutes. Watch the yeast start to bubble and froth!

4 Pour the flour into a large bowl. Stir in the salt and sunflower oil.

5 Pour in the yeast and water mixture and stir with a wooden spoon.

6 When the mixture sticks together in a ball, put it onto the table. Knead it well with your hands for about ten minutes to make the dough smooth and springy. You might need some extra flour so the dough doesn't stick to the table.

7 Put the dough in a clean bowl. Cover it with clingfilm and leave it in a warm place for about 1 hour to rise. Watch it grow!

8 When the dough has doubled in size, take it out of the bowl and knead it again for five minutes.

9 Cut it into 12 pieces and shape each piece into a ball. Put the balls on a baking tray. Cover them and leave them to rise again for about 20 minutes.

10 Meanwhile, turn on the oven to 200ºC/400ºF/ Gas mark 6.

11 When the rolls have doubled in size, bake them for about 20 minutes until they are golden brown.

12 Put the rolls on a wire rack to cool.

Makes 12 rolls
Preparation time:
1½ hours
Cooking time:
40 minutes

Ingredients:
25g dried yeast
1 teaspoon sugar
225ml warm water
375g wholemeal flour
1 tablespoon sunflower oil

Equipment:
Large bowl
Measuring jug
Teaspoon
Tablespoon
Clingfilm
Baking tray

THE OVEN, THE BAKING TRAY AND THE ROLLS WILL BE VERY HOT. DO NOT TOUCH ! ASK AN ADULT!

statement of purpose

important to know how many recipe makes before deciding to use it

useful to know if you have enough time for this recipe

makes bread rise

healthier than white

made from sunflower seeds

what you need, listed in columns in the order items are added/used

numbered steps

big, bold, full capitals with exclamation marks so there is no missing the safety warning

Route map

from *Discovery World Stage F: Maps*

Background

This pictorial text develops map-reading skills and directional vocabulary. The map is a simple bird's-eye view of part of a town with a route marked by arrows. The context will be familiar to children, as will many of the buildings, which are labelled. The map can be used as a starting point for describing routes, using appropriate vocabulary. These can be written as a set of directions, exploring key features of this particular type of instructional text, including steps in chronological order with appropriate connectives and the use of imperatives. The text has links to geography and maths and could also be related to work on road safety.

What's on the CD-ROM

The CD-ROM contains the same map as the core text but without the labels. This means that less able readers can use the map and view the route with fewer reading demands. To help the children understand the map they could add their own labels.

Discussing the text

● Display the text and ask the children to identify what it is. Share experiences of using maps. If possible, display various different types of map.

● Ensure the children understand that a map or plan is a bird's-eye view and represents objects and buildings in simple ways, without detail. (This understanding may need to have been developed earlier during geography work.)

● Read the introduction and ask children to point to *Lucy and John's house* and the *school*. Ask a child to trace with a finger their route from home to school.

● Then ask children to find other buildings or streets marked on the map. (You might point out that cars are not usually shown on maps because they are not always there.) Ask them to talk about similar places in their own towns to ensure shared understanding.

● Annotate the map to identify key features such as: *tree, building, pond, path, road, route*. Then collate these to produce a key to the map. Show keys on other maps to help with this.

● Begin to describe the route shown on the map. (It may be helpful to use a large copy of the map on the floor to assist understanding of direction. Take opportunities to consider road safety issues.) In shared writing, construct, first orally then in writing, a description of the route. Use time connectives and directional vocabulary and mention key features passed.

● Tell the children that you are now going to turn the description of the route into a set of directions (instructions) that will tell someone else how to get from the house to the school. Model sentences such as: *First come out of the house and turn left. Now walk to the end of the road. Cross the road on the zebra crossing.* Highlight the imperatives, referring the children to earlier work on instructions.

● Now annotate key features of the text constructed – aim, time connectives, imperatives, directional vocabulary, names of places passed – and display this for reference.

Talk, read and write

● Ask the children, in pairs, to mark routes between other places on the map and then write directions, using the list of features compiled earlier. These can be swapped with others to follow and evaluate.

● Use play mats or layouts made from construction kits to practise directional vocabulary and give directions to each other.

● Give the children directions around school to follow. They can then make up their own routes and write, or record on tape, directions for others to follow. If a map or plan of the school is available, children could mark routes on this.

● Construct an illustrated glossary of directional vocabulary, including: *left, right, straight on, past, along, next to, turn*.

Extension

Ask children to pay close attention to their route from home to school (or vice versa). They can note the important buildings that they pass, and the directions they take. Ask parents or carers to help to mark their routes on a local street map (copyright permitting) and write directions. Use other opportunities as they arise to follow and write directions.

2: 1: T17: to use diagrams in instructions

2: 1: W10: to learn new words from reading linked to particular topics

school gate must be here

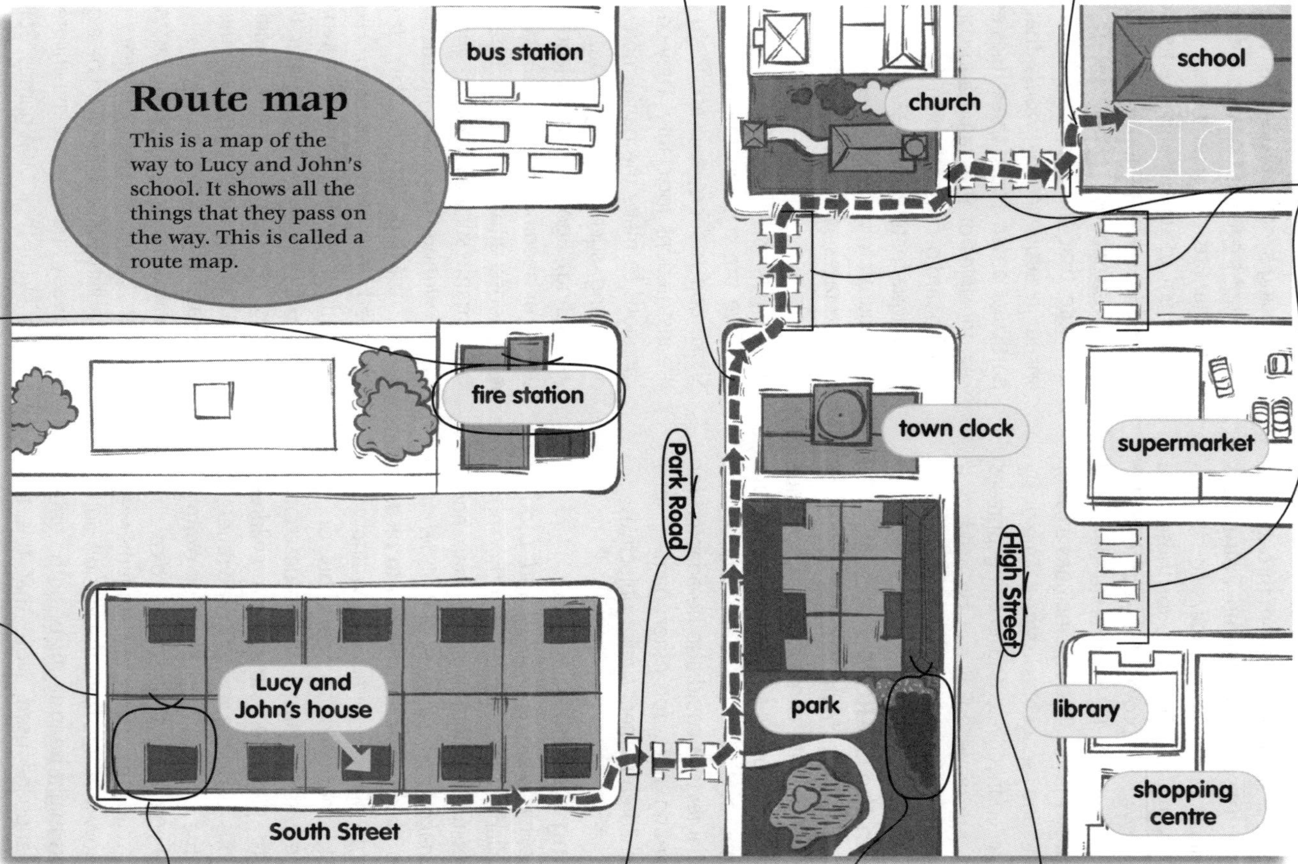

Lucy and John take the safe place to cross – zebra crossing

school

supermarket

shopping centre

library

High Street

often used for a town's main street, where shops and banks are

church

town clock

park

trees shown because they are big and would be seen from road

Park Road

arrows show direction John and Lucy take

bus station

fire station

so-called because the park is in it

Route map

This is a map of the way to Lucy and John's school. It shows all the things that they pass on the way. This is called a route map.

Lucy and John's house

South Street

label

simplified plan view of houses, no detail

individual trees and plants in gardens not shown because they are small

Text and illustrations "Discovery World Stage F: Maps" © 1997, Reed Educational and Professional Publishing Ltd. Illustrations Roger Fereday/Linda Rogers Associates

2: 1: S5: to revise knowledge about other uses of capitalisation

2: 1: T15: to write simple instructions

2: 1: S6: to use a variety of simple organisational devices

Snakes and ladders
by Sue Taylor

Background
Many children will have played traditional board games, including *Snakes and Ladders*. Often, they will have learned to play them through oral instructions. This text of written instructions can introduce *Snakes and Ladders* to children unfamiliar with the game, and, for those who already know it, provide a context for comparison between their understanding and this particular version. The text includes a list of equipment and sequenced steps linked by appropriate connectives, and exciting phrases that draw the reader in. It can be used as a model for writing rules for other games.

What's on the CD-ROM
This text is a writing frame for instructions of the same game, with connectives as sentence starters. It can help less able readers to explore key features of the layout and language of instructional texts. It could also be adapted for use in writing rules for other games, thus enabling children to meet similar objectives.

Discussing the text
● If possible have a *Snakes and Ladders* board available and a display of other board games. Begin by asking children to talk about playing *Snakes and Ladders*, and how they learned to play it. Ask the children to recall in pairs how to play the game. (If few know the game, ask one child to share his or her knowledge with the class.) Write a description of how to play the game from children's contributions, using the *you* form and reflecting some of the spoken language, for example: *Well, what you do is, you throw the dice…*

● Now read the core text together and consider how it differs from the version on the board. This might be in terms of both content and the language used. Note that this text instructs people how to play, rather than describes how one person plays. Key differences to consider are the use of subheadings (to add clarity and organisation), connectives (to indicate chronological order), imperatives (the 'bossy' language) and more concise expression (such as the complex sentences explaining the snakes and the ladders). Discuss the role of the picture in helping readers to 'see' what is going on in the text.

● Identify and label key features of the text: the title (goal/aim), introductory sentences, equipment needed, sequence of instructions, and closing sentence. Consider whether any of the sections could be read in a different order. Note the use of bullet points for the list of equipment to separate the items. Ask children to consider whether numbers would add clarity to the instructions.

● Note that the first three instructions are linked in sequence by words that suggest a particular order. These three rules establish the key principles of the game and could apply to other board games. The next two sentences are the unique features of *Snakes and Ladders*. Ask the children to consider the effect of the smiley and sad faces as a visual shorthand.

Talk, read and write
● Give the children the opportunity to play *Snake and Ladders*, and ask them to evaluate the instructions for clarity. They could suggest variations to make the game more challenging or exciting, such as using two dice (adding or subtracting), going down ladders and up snakes or needing an exact number to finish.

● Choose another familiar board game (or simple game such as *Noughts and Crosses*). In shared writing, compose instructions for this game, drawing on the key text features identified in shared reading. Highlight the imperatives and list these as a word bank for children's own writing. Consider the value of pictures or diagrams and additional, non-instructional, phrases to engage the reader and encourage him or her to play.

● Children can now write instructions for another game of their choice, perhaps in mixed-ability pairs. This could be a game which they already know, but some children might be able to invent their own games. Some children can work in a guided group and may need to play a game and write the rules as they play.

● Instructions can then be swapped so children can play games according to each other's rules. How successful are they?

Extension
Children can bring in games from home, with accompanying instructions. Ask them to read aloud the instructions for others to follow.

2: 1: T13: to read simple written instructions

2: 1: T15: to write simple instructions

2: 1: S2: to find examples of words and phrases that link sentences

picture useful for quickly seeing what text is about, and for readers who don't already know the game

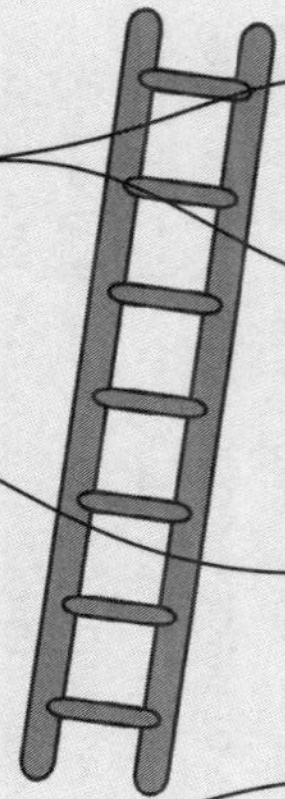

sequenced instructions, using sequential time connectives

good thing because you jump over lots of squares and move up board quicker

bad thing because you slide back down the board

final, bold 'instruction' catches the eye and makes game sound exciting and thrilling

Text © 2007, Sue Taylor

SNAKES AND LADDERS

100	99	98	97	96	95	94	93	92	91
81	82	83	84	85	86	87	88	89	90
80	79	78	77	76	75	74	73	72	71
61	62	63	64	65	66	67	68	69	70
60	59	58	57	56	55	54	53	52	51
41	42	43	44	45	46	47	48	49	50
40	39	38	37	36	35	34	33	32	31
21	22	23	24	25	26	27	28	29	30
20	19	18	17	16	15	14	13	12	11
1	2	3	4	5	6	7	8	9	10

How to play Snakes and Ladders

This is a game for 2–4 players (keeps you busy at wet playtime!)

This is what you need

- one snakes and ladders board
- one dice
- a counter for each player

How to play

First, put all the counters on the first square (number 1).

Then, throw the dice to decide who will go first. The highest number starts.

Now, take it in turns to throw the dice and move your counter the number of spaces that the dice shows.

If you land on the bottom of a ladder, go straight up it to the top.

If you land on the head of a snake, go right down to its tail.

The winner is the first person to get to the last square (number 100).

HAVE FUN AND WATCH OUT FOR THOSE SNAKES!

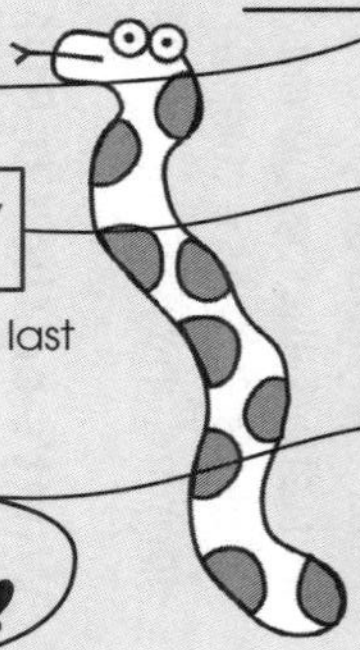

goal of text given in title

'2 to 4', ie, game can be played by 2, 3 or 4 players

tagline entices reader, invites him or her to play

subheadings

equipment given in easy-to-see bulleted list

imperatives near the start of sentence or clause

the instruction comes in second part of sentence and depends on the 'if' in first part (what happens)

how the game ends

2: 1: T3: to be aware of the difference between spoken and written language

2: 1: T14: to note key structural features, such as clear statement of purpose at start, sequential steps set out in a list, direct language

2: 1: T16: to use models from reading to organise instructions sequentially

How to play hopscotch

by Sue Taylor

Background

Hopscotch is a traditional playground game, still popular with children. It requires few resources and encourages children to be active at playtime. This text provides written instructions for the game. It demonstrates key features of the instructional genre, including a list of equipment needed, numbered sequential instructions, time connectives and imperative verbs. Diagrams support the written steps. The text offers the opportunity to read and write numbers to ten or twenty, and the actions of hopping and jumping can be practice for PE.

What's on the CD-ROM

This writing frame uses the time connectives from the core text as sentence starters. It has been simplified to just four steps that provide the key principles of playing the game. Children could add further instructions for developing the game if appropriate. It can be used in guided sessions to reinforce the structure and language of instructional texts, using the diagrams as visual prompts. It could also be adapted to provide a starting point for writing instructions for a different game.

Discussing the text

● Read the text and share children's experiences of playing *hopscotch* and how they learned to play. If possible, take the children into the playground or large indoor space and organise groups to play the game. Include one confident writer as a note-taker in each group. Even if children know the game, tell them to follow the instructions. Some assistance may be needed in understanding the diagrams as a bird's-eye view of the grid and the position of the player in relation to it. Numbers can be written as figures or words as appropriate.

● Back in the classroom, ask groups to evaluate the effectiveness of the instructions, using notes taken during play. Share experiences and encourage suggestions for improvement if needed. Children who are familiar with the game might offer additions or variations.

● Encourage children to pick out typical genre features of the text. Discuss the purpose of each part and whether any parts could be re-ordered. Note that instructions 1 to 4 set out the key principles of playing the game, step 5

adds the element of competition and excitement and 6 offers an adaptation.

● Consider the use of the bulleted list for equipment. Rewrite the same list as a sentence with items separated by commas. Which is easier to read?

● Look closely at the written instructions and consider which would be difficult to interpret without the diagrams. Test whether the diagrams alone would be effective.

● Highlight the words and phrases at the beginning of each instruction that provide the chronological link. Note how these reinforce the order the steps must be carried out.

● Focus on the imperatives in the first two instructions. Elicit that these are the words that tell the player what to do. Ask the children to find the other imperatives in the text.

● Use the opportunity to reinforce reading and spelling of numbers to ten and twenty.

Talk, read and write

● Choose another familiar playground game and use shared writing to compose a set of instructions, using the features identified earlier. Discuss the value of diagrams to support the written text and further suggestions that might be included to engage the reader. Ensure that this model is clearly displayed and that key features are identified and labelled.

● Children can now work independently (or in pairs) to write instructions for another game of their choice. Ensure that they refer to the model from shared writing. Encourage them to include diagrams where they would be helpful. If space and time are available, children can then swap their instructions and play each other's games. Writing frames may be needed by some children.

● Practise reading and spelling of numbers using sequencing cards and matching words to numbers.

Extension

Ask children to talk to family members about the games they played at school. Provide a writing frame and encourage children to write instructions for one game described. They can then use these to teach others in class to play the new game.

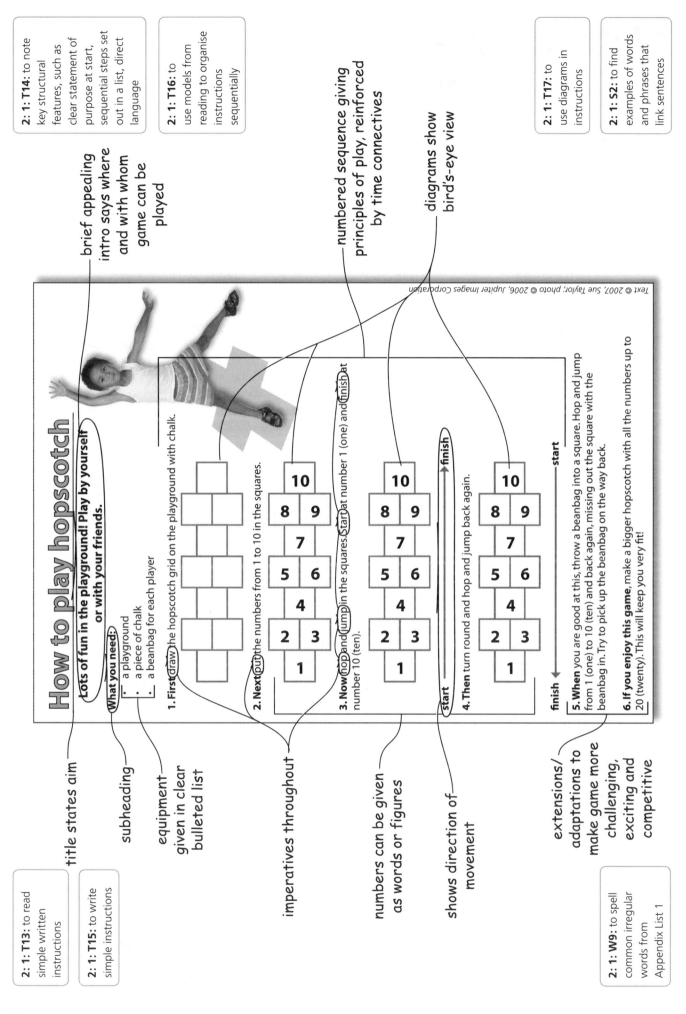

2: 1: T14: to note key structural features, such as clear statement of purpose at start, sequential steps set out in a list, direct language

2: 1: T16: to use models from reading to organise instructions sequentially

2: 1: T17: to use diagrams in instructions

2: 1: S2: to find examples of words and phrases that link sentences

2: 1: T13: to read simple written instructions

2: 1: T15: to write simple instructions

2: 1: W9: to spell common irregular words from Appendix List 1

brief appealing intro says where and with whom game can be played

numbered sequence giving principles of play, reinforced by time connectives

diagrams show bird's-eye view

title states aim

subheading

equipment given in clear bulleted list

imperatives throughout

numbers can be given as words or figures

shows direction of movement

extensions/ adaptations to make game more challenging, exciting and competitive

How to play hopscotch

Lots of fun in the playground! Play by yourself or with your friends.

What you need:
- a playground
- a piece of chalk
- a beanbag for each player

1. First draw the hopscotch grid on the playground with chalk.

2. Next put the numbers from 1 to 10 in the squares.

3. Now hop and jump in the squares. Start at number 1 (one) and finish at number 10 (ten).

4. Then turn round and hop and jump back again.

5. When you are good at this, throw a beanbag into a square. Hop and jump from 1 (one) to 10 (ten) and back again, missing out the square with the beanbag in. Try to pick up the beanbag on the way back.

6. If you enjoy this game, make a bigger hopscotch with all the numbers up to 20 (twenty). This will keep you very fit!

start

finish

Text © 2007, Sue Taylor; photo © 2006, Jupiter Images Corporation

String games — cup and saucer
by Sue Taylor

Background

Across the world people have used string pictures as part of storytelling, turning an ordinary piece of string into a picture of something in their everyday lives. For example, the Arctic Inuit made reindeer and wolves out of string, while the Navajo knew how to make coyotes and owls. Many children will have played *Cat's Cradle* or made pictures with string and most will have learned through copying others. This text offers written instructions for making one 'picture'. Each step is clearly illustrated and the text highlights the value of diagrams to support written text, and vice versa. Ideally, you will need a piece of string 1½ metres long for each child.

What's on the CD-ROM

The activity is presented using the same illustrations and a writing frame that uses time connectives as sentence starters. Less able readers will be able to play the game using the diagrams and oral instructions. In guided writing children can compose their own instructions, using the frame, which enables them to explore the structure and language of instructional texts.

Discussing the text

● Before introducing the text, encourage the children to share their understanding and experience of string games, pictures or *Cat's Cradle*. Provide some background information about string pictures, as above.

● Ask children who have played these games how they learned them, then explain that this text is a written set of instructions that explains how to make one picture.

● Give each child a piece of string and ask them to follow your instructions. (Those who have played before should try to do only what you tell them to do.) Read the text aloud, without showing the pictures, and evaluate the outcomes. It is likely that some children will have been unsuccessful; discuss the difficulties.

● Now reveal the pictures, one at a time (keeping the writing hidden) or give children copies. Ask them to try again, using the pictures only. Compare this with the previous attempt. Which was more successful and why?

● Now reveal the complete text. Carry out the activity again, this time reading the text and exploring pictures carefully. Demonstrate steps if necessary. Most children should be successful this time; consider why it was easier.

● Discuss what makes a set of instructions easy to follow, drawing out the value of written text and illustrations to support each other. Children might consider that in fact the easiest way to learn is to be shown by an expert.

● Highlight the words that indicate the actions to be taken (the imperatives), noting that they are usually placed at the beginning of the sentence. Identify the exceptions, noting the time connectives that reinforce the sequence of the steps and, in step 7, the additional information about how to carry out the action. Identify other places where additional explanations are given to clarify the main instructions.

Talk, read and write

● Ask the children to share their knowledge of games they learned to play through oral instructions or by watching others. Agree on one to use in shared writing, and compose a written set of instructions. Then establish where diagrams might be useful. Annotate the text produced to identify key features, including imperatives and connectives to reinforce the sequence of actions.

● Now ask the children to choose their own game and to give instructions orally to a partner before writing them down, adding illustrations. Remind them to use the model from shared writing. The pairs can act as response partners to check each other's talk and writing against the features identified earlier and for sense and punctuation. Less able learners could work in guided groups. Encourage more able learners to add detail to ensure clarity and precision.

● Now ask the pairs to swap their instructions with new pairs and to follow and evaluate the instructions, noting good points and suggesting improvements where appropriate.

Extension

Ask children to find different types of instructions in the classroom or at home and categorise them. These can be labelled and displayed to illustrate the importance of instructions in a range of different contexts.

2: 1: T15: to write simple instructions

2: 1: S4: to re-read own writing for sense and punctuation

2: 1: T13: to read simple written instructions

2: 1: T18: to use appropriate register in writing instructions

only one item needed, given in a full sentence, with no subheading

time connectives reinforce sequence

simple imperative verbs

additional information so reader can check progress

in bold as this is the goal/ achievement

numbered sequence of steps – simple, short sentences

pictures support understanding of text

additional explanation clarifies instruction

String Games
Cup and Saucer

You will need a piece of string about 1½ metres long, with the ends tied **together to make a loop.**

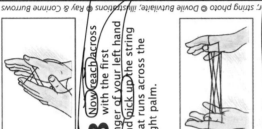

1 Loop the string across both of your palms and behind your little fingers and thumbs.

2 Now reach across with the first finger of your right hand and pick up the string that runs across the left palm. Pull your hands apart.

3 Now reach across with the first finger of your left hand and pick up the string that runs across the right palm.

4 Pull your hands apart again.

5 Next reach over with both thumbs and hook them under the string on the far side of each first finger.

6 Pull your thumbs back to where they started from. You will have two loops on each thumb.

7 Using your mouth or your other hand, pull the bottom loops off your thumbs. These loops will have to pass over the top ones to come off.

8 Now drop the loops from both little fingers and pull your hands apart.

9 Tilt your thumbs up so the **Cup and Saucer** are right-side up.

Text © 2007, Sue Taylor; string photo © Dovile Butvilaite; illustrations © Ray & Corinne Burrows

Mixing colours

by Sue Taylor

Background

This text links to art and design and provides instructions for obtaining secondary colours from primary colours and then using them to paint a rainbow. You will need to explain that the colours of a real rainbow are made when light splits and that the colours are not quite the same as when paint is mixed. Rainbows in the sky have seven colours (which children might know), whereas paint mixing in this way only produces six. The instructions include the goal in the title, a list of materials and equipment needed, steps for mixing paints, and supplementary background information. Unlike many instructional texts, some of the steps could be re-ordered. Key technical vocabulary is included, and where instructions are repeated the language is varied to develop children's knowledge. The text provides a meaningful opportunity for reinforcing reading and spelling of colours.

What's on the CD-ROM

The differentiated text is a simplified set of instructions for the same activity. It is predominantly visual, with minimal written text, to enable less able readers to engage with the practical activity with fewer reading demands. Typical genre features are retained, including the list of materials and equipment, key imperatives and some technical vocabulary. After carrying out the activity, children could work in groups to compose additional text, using the pictures as a starting point.

Discussing the text

● Show and read just the title and establish the children's understanding of colours and rainbows. Discuss, at an appropriate level, the difference between a rainbow in the sky, and one that is created on paper with paint.

● Explain that the text is a set of instructions, and share experiences of using other types of instructions in the classroom and at home.

● Reveal and read the *What you need* section and ask why this section comes first. Consider the advantages of a list with items below each other.

● Now read the sentences that provide background information. Discuss the technical vocabulary *primary* and *secondary*, relating it perhaps to primary (first) and secondary (second) school, and note which of the six rainbow colours are in which category.

● Reveal the first instruction and the illustration with it. Discuss the significance of *First* and *put*. Note the additional instruction about washing the brush.

● Uncover and read the next written instruction, this time without revealing the illustration. Identify again the imperatives and brush-washing instruction, draw attention to the variation in language. Ask the children to predict what colour will be produced (reminding them of the secondary colours identified earlier).

● Reveal the illustrations, and read them as a word sum, checking understanding of the symbols + and =.

● Reveal the rest of the instructions one part at a time, and, as above, discuss significant features of the language and layout.

● Notice how the last sentences refer the reader back to the original goal and give the activity a purpose.

● If possible, cut and move parts of the text and consider the effect of re-ordering. Elicit that in some cases this does not matter. Compare this to other instructions, such as recipes, where the order of steps is crucial.

Talk, read and write

● Allow the children to carry out the activity and evaluate the instructions.

● Some children could make large posters for the art area, perhaps using the 'word sum' format. Encourage them to include short captions, using the direct language of instructions. Remind them to include an additional reminder for washing brushes.

● Practise reading and spelling the colours. Encourage them to match colour cards to words, and use appropriate strategies such as Look-Say-Cover-Write-Check. Then ask the children to label their rainbows for display.

Extension

For homework, ask children to draw and colour a picture that contains each of the primary and secondary colours. Ask them to label the colours or write sentences about their picture that include the colour words.

MIXING COLOURS TO PAINT A RAINBOW

WHAT YOU NEED:
Red, yellow and blue paint
6 clean pots to put paint in
A thick paintbrush
A pot of clean water
A big piece of paper to paint a rainbow

Yellow, red and blue are called the **primary colours**. When you mix two primary colours, you get the secondary colours.

First put some **yellow**, **red** and **blue** paint in three separate pots. Don't forget to wash your brush before you put it into a different colour.

To make **orange** paint, take some of the yellow paint and put it in another pot. Wash your brush in clean water. Now add some red paint to this new pot of yellow and mix well. What colour do you get?

YELLOW + RED = ORANGE

To make **green** paint, take some more of the yellow paint and put it in another clean pot. (Remember to wash your brush every time you use a new colour.) Add some blue paint and mix well. What colour is it?

YELLOW + BLUE = GREEN

To make **purple** paint, put some blue paint in the last clean pot. (Wash your brush!) Add some red paint and mix. What colour do you see?

BLUE + RED = PURPLE

You now have six colours – **red**, **yellow**, **orange**, **green**, **blue** and **purple**. These are the colours of the rainbow.
Paint a big rainbow like the one in the picture at the top.

Text © 2007, Sue Taylor

Annotations:

2: 1: T14: to note key structural features, such as clear statement of purpose at start, sequential steps set out in a list, direct language

2: 1: W9: to spell common irregular words from Appendix List 1

negative imperative – tells reader what not to do

imperatives – language addresses reader directly

direct questions require further involvement from reader

final step to fully achieve goal

2: 1: S6: to use a variety of simple organisational devices to indicate sequences and relationships

2: 1: T13: to read simple written instructions

title says what reader can learn from text

listed clearly; given first so reader can gather everything ready

technical vocabulary given in background introduction

identifies starting point...

...but sequence of these steps doesn't matter – separate goals

takes reader back to beginning of text and original aim

2: 1: W10: to learn new words from reading linked to particular topics

Painting butterflies
by Sue Taylor

Background

This text can be used in conjunction with the previous one on mixing paint colours. Both demonstrate key structural features of instructional texts, including the goal, list of materials needed and sequenced steps. This text, however, addresses the reader using *you* rather than giving direct orders with the imperative, creating a friendlier tone. This style can be compared to that of the previous text or other instructions, and can be changed to explore the differences. The text ties in with work in science on invertebrates or life cycles and with symmetry in maths.

What's on the CD-ROM

This is a writing frame for the same activity, providing key structural features as starting points for less able readers and writers. After children have carried out the activity, guided writing will enable them to explore the structure of instructional texts. In groups, they could write instructions, using either the imperative form or the less formal *you*, or change the former to the latter to explore the differences. The frame could also be adapted to provide the structure for instructions in other contexts.

Discussing the text

● If possible have a finished butterfly on display. Read the text and encourage the children to share any experiences of this method of painting. Draw on their understanding of symmetry as appropriate.

● Together, identify, label and discuss the purpose of each part of the text: title, picture, list of materials, numbered instructions, closing sentences (which offer 'optional extras'; explain the meaning of *antennae* if necessary).

● Read the list of materials needed, considering the layout and why it comes first in the text. Show an example of *A4 paper.* Talk about the purpose of the additional information provided for the number of brushes needed, the type of paint and number of colours.

● Read the instructions, noting the numbers and time connectives, reinforcing the sequence. You could ask children to visualise, or mime the actions as you read and to comment on the clarity of the written text. Consider whether pictures at each stage would be useful.

● Note how the writer directly addresses the reader, *you*, which makes the text sound personal. It would be helpful to compare this with an instructional text shared previously that uses imperatives. Note the difference in tone: the imperative sounds 'bossy', but makes the actions required absolutely clear.

● Focus on word-level learning by highlighting the *s* that indicates plural in *colours* and *blobs*. Brainstorm other words that add *s* for plural, noting that it sometimes sounds like 'z', but is always written with the letter *s*. Now look at *butterfly/butterflies* and point out how the spelling changes. Practise with other examples of *y*-ending nouns that change to *ie* before adding *s*. Deal with exceptions such as *monkey* that follow their own rule. Also explore the plural of *brush*, noting the 'iz' sound.

Talk, read and write

● Ask the children to find in the first instruction the words that tell the reader what to do (*fold* and *open*). Use shared writing to model how to turn this sentence into a direct instruction by deleting the unnecessary words (*you need to*). Repeat if necessary with the next instruction. Then ask the children to continue independently to rewrite the instructions.

● Ask groups to discuss which style they prefer and why. This could be reinforced through other contexts, such as building simple models from construction kits and then telling others how to do it, using the two different styles. Some children might consider the appropriateness of each style according to the audience.

● After carrying out the activity, ask the children to add any illustrations they think would support and clarify the written text.

● Help the children to explore and record different ways of pluralising, using suitable dictionaries.

Extension

Ask children to write a set of instructions for a simple activity they do at home, such as getting dressed or laying the table. Some children might do this in the two different styles explored above; others might need a writing frame or could draw a sequence of pictures with captions.

Text © 2007, Sue Taylor

Painting butterflies

2: 1: T14: to note key structural features, such as clear statement of purpose at start, sequential steps set out in a list, direct language

2: 1: S2: to find examples of words and phrases that link sentences

plural spelling 'y' changes to 'i' and 'es' added

present tense verbs – would be imperatives in more direct text

direct address to reader; gives slightly different tone to direct imperatives

'feelers'

numbered sequence, reinforced by time connectives

extra display idea will give impression of butterflies flying

You will need:
A piece of plain (A4) paper
Thick paintbrushes – one for each colour of paint that you use
Paint (thick paint made from powder is best, or poster paint from a bottle. You will need about 4 bright colours)
A pot of clean water
An apron

1. First you need to fold the paper in half and then open it out again.

2. Next you put blobs of different coloured paint on one side of the paper.

3. Then you need to fold the paper in half again, with the paint inside. You can press the paper together and rub your hand across the paper to spread the paint inside.

4. Now you can open up the paper again and look at your butterfly.

You could add a body and antennae. If you cut out your butterfly you can hang it up in the classroom.

subject-specific term for certain size of paper

plural spelling 'es' added

each brush can then stay in its own pot

tools and materials to organise before starting

depends on personal choice and how things go

personal tone

2: 1: T13: to read simple written instructions

2: 1: W7: to use word endings such as 's' (plural) to support their reading and spelling

How to look after a hamster by Sue Taylor

Background

Most young children are interested in animals and many will own a pet. You might have a class or school pet. The citizenship curriculum emphasises the importance of children learning to take responsibility, including for animal welfare. This text presents simple instructions to help children understand the demands of being a pet owner, and it demonstrates many key features of this genre. There is a list of equipment required, and simple, direct language is used, including imperatives. Items are set out in bulleted lists for clarity, and pictures support the written text. Additional advice for the new pet owner is included after dashes. Unlike many instructions, these do not need to be followed in a particular order.

What's on the CD-ROM

This is a simpler version of the same text. The additional advice is omitted to help less able readers to engage with the key ideas with fewer reading demands. The same pictures are included and children could use the list of items to label these. The list of instructions could be used as a cloze text, with imperatives omitted for example, in guided group work.

Discussing the text

- Show and read the title and introduction and look at the top picture. Encourage the children to talk about experiences of looking after pets, including the class pet if applicable. Who has pets? Who looks after them? What do their pets need? Discuss the fun that can be had but also the important responsibility, noting that the introduction makes this clear.
- What kind of text do children think this is? Reveal the rest to confirm that it is a set of instructions. Identify the two key parts of the text – what you need and what to do.
- Read the first section, noting the bullet points that list each item clearly. Notice how the bottom picture helps the reader to understand what hamster equipment might look like. Encourage any hamster owners to suggest any other items needed. Does it matter in which order the items are listed? Consider the purpose of the additional information given after the dashes and discuss the effect of omitting this.
- Read and discuss the *What you need to do*

section, again noting the bullet points. Would it matter if the list was in a different order? Some children might suggest an order of importance, but note that the instructions are not 'steps' and that one is not dependent on a previous one.
- Ask the children why the author has included the last sentence. Note that it is a direct appeal to the reader.
- Highlight *Put* and *Clean* and revise the 'bossy' function of these words. Ask children to highlight other imperatives. Notice their position at the beginning of each instruction, and point out the emphatic effect of *Always* in the final point.

Talk, read and write

- If there are enough pet owners, spread them out in groups to describe to other children how they look after their pets. If not, ask some children to describe to the class, or you can take the role yourself.
- Choose one pet and, in shared writing, list items needed using bullet points as in the text. Write what to do as a set of notes, again using bullets. Model how to turn the notes into a sentence, using appropriate instructional language.
- Now ask the children to use this model to complete a set of instructions in independent writing. Some might choose their own pet or one that another child has described and more able writers could include additional advice for the reader. Use response partners to check for sense and punctuation. Less able readers and writers might draw and label diagrams, and compose instructions in guided writing.
- Provide a range of instructional texts for groups to explore and identify common features and significant differences. Ask them to compare layout, structure and language.

Extension

Pet owners could bring in photographs of their pets, and books and leaflets about their care to create a display.

Ask children to make posters to describe the needs of *all* pets, drawing on experiences shared in class (for example, food, water, shelter, exercise, care).

2: 1: T14: to note key structural features

2: 1: T15: to write simple instructions

helps to identify subject

not in sequence, order is not important and no step follows or is dependent on any other

eg, not near a radiator, in the sun or in a draft

you could do this more often, but never less

short imperative verbs at beginning of sentence each time

2: 1: T17: to use diagrams in instructions

2: 1: T18: to use appropriate register in writing instructions

forceful time connective; this point is very important

Text © 2007, Sue Taylor; photos © Photodisc Inc

How to look after a hamster

Before buying a hamster, ask for advice from a pet shop or a vet and buy a book about hamsters.

Hamsters can be fun but they need to be cared for.

You will need:

• A hamster cage – it must be spacious, have a nestbox and be escape-proof.
• A food container – it must be quite heavy so that it can't be tipped over easily.
• A water container – upside-down bottles are best.
• Exercise ladders or wheels – so your hamster doesn't get too fat or lazy!
• Bedding – straw or hay sold in your pet shop is best.
• Floor covering – you can buy sawdust or woodshavings from the pet shop.
• Food – seeds and nuts, fruit and vegetables.

What you need to do:

• Put the cage somewhere not too hot and not too cold.
• Clean out the cage at least once a week.
• Feed your hamster once a day.
• Wash the food bowl every day.
• Give your hamster fresh water every day.
• Always handle your hamster gently and carefully.

Look after your hamster well and you will have lots of fun together!

encouraging closing line

2: 1: T13: to read simple written instructions

tells reader what text will help him or her to do

introduction gives important general advice

why you might want one (pictures also contribute to this)

the responsibility that comes with them

subheading followed by bulleted points

specific detail given after the dash for each item highlights importance of getting the correct things

2: 1: W10: to learn new words from reading linked to particular topics

2: 1: S4: to re-read own writing for sense and punctuation.

Making sentences with Roamer
by Valiant Technology

Background

Children will be learning to program devices such as a floor turtle in ICT. This may be linked to work with maps and directions in geography and shape and space in maths. This text provides a set of sequential instructions, using the imperative, to program a Roamer to move forwards and backwards and to wait. This work can be used to collect words to produce sentences, providing a meaningful context for, and reinforcing understanding of, sentences. Roamer can be pre-programmed to define the length of its 'steps' (and, for other programs, the unit of turn – such as a right angle). For this set of instructions, it is probably appropriate to define the Roamer 'step' as 10cm by pressing *CM CM ^ [ ] 1 0 [ ] GO*. The definition will be retained until Roamer is switched off.

What's on the CD-ROM

This is a set of instructions to program Roamer to carry out one simple task. As in the core text, Roamer will be programmed to move forwards and backwards and to wait. The instructions are presented as written text, using imperatives, and combining sequences of Roamer symbols. With support, less able readers will be able to engage with the language of instructions, matching written text to Roamer keys, and can use this model to write their own instructions in guided work.

Discussing the text

● Pre-program Roamer to carry out a sequence of movements. Begin the lesson by observing it in action. Ask the children how Roamer knows where to go. (It is carrying out a set of instructions that you gave it.)

● Discuss other types of instructions that the children are familiar with. Then show this text and explain that it is a set of instructions to program Roamer. Demonstrate how Roamer is given instructions and explore the keys.

● Note that the text's title suggests a possible activity using Roamer, and draw attention to the capital letter for the machine's name.

● Read the first instruction, asking a child to carry it out. Ask the children to identify the imperative.

● Read the next two instructions, checking understanding of vocabulary. Notice how the symbols in the text match the keys on Roamer. Ask a child to press the forward key, and explain why nothing happens (because Roamer needs to know *how far* to go).

● Identify the use of *n* to represent *number* in the next instruction. Explain that the *programmer* decides how far he or she wants Roamer to go and presses appropriate numbers. Program Roamer to go forwards, using a number between one and ten. Observe the relative distances using other numbers. Repeat this to explore waiting time, using the *w* key.

● Read the penultimate sentence, which refers the reader back to the title. Explore the words at the bottom of the page and ask the children to imagine what the girl in the picture is doing with Roamer. Set up a line of words from the suggestions, for example, *you make me laugh.* Can children make other sentences using the words given.

● Read the final instruction, explaining the importance of the *CM (Cancel Memory)* key. Discuss the position of this instruction and consider whether it is in the best place.

Talk, read and write

● Encourage small groups to use trial and error to program Roamer to make sentences. Then model how to write each instruction as children achieve success, using imperatives as in the text. Ask the children to write instructions to make different sentences and swap them with others' to try.

● Model writing an instruction as a sequence of keys, such as *CM CM ^ 2*. Ask the children to rewrite their instructions in this way, using a new line for each step. Again, children should try each other's programs.

● Ask the children to explore and write programs for different tasks, such as navigating an obstacle course using the 'turn' keys.

● Some children could go on to make classroom posters to show others how to use Roamer, labelling the keys.

Extension

Give children differentiated sets of words and ask them to write instructions for making different sentences, using the models explored. They can use their instructions to program Roamer and evaluate their success.

Making sentences with Roamer

- capital letter for brand name
- nothing happens until Roamer is told how far to go
- picture adds clarity
- sequential steps
- links to picture
- should this instruction come earlier?

- something you can make Roamer do
- imperatives – direct, impersonal language
- symbols match those on Roamer
- stands for 'number' – programmer sets units of movement
- stands for 'wait'
- more personal; involves reader
- stands for 'Cancel Memory' (deletes previous instructions)

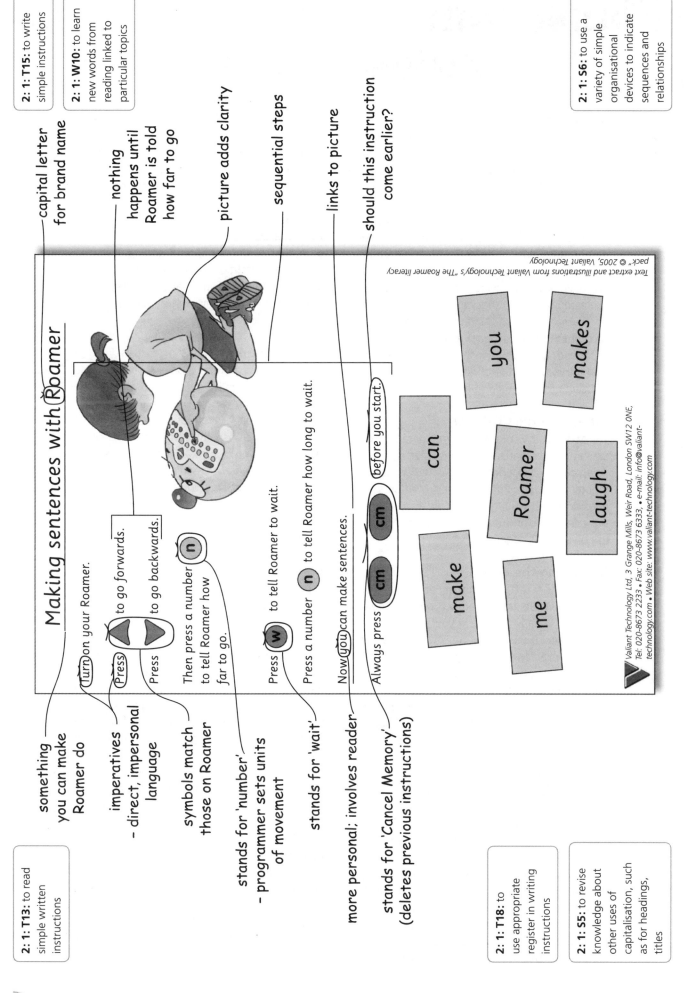

Turn on your Roamer.

Press ▶ to go forwards.

Press ◀ to go backwards.

Then press a number (n) to tell Roamer how far to go.

Press (w) to tell Roamer to wait.

Press a number (n) to tell Roamer how long to wait.

Now you can make sentences.

Always press (cm)(cm) before you start.

you   makes   can   Roamer   laugh   make   me

Text extract and illustrations from Valiant Technology's "The Roamer literacy pack." © 2005, Valiant Technology

Valiant Technology Ltd, 3 Grange Mills, Weir Road, London SW12 0NE; Tel: 020-8673 2233 • Fax: 020-8673 6333. • e-mail: info@valiant-technology.com • Web site: www.valiant-technology.com

Classroom rules  by Sue Taylor

Background

School and class rules will be a very familiar context for the children. This text presents a set of rules for an imaginary class. It provides an opportunity for discussing the reasons for rules in different contexts. The text could be used at the beginning of the school year as a starting point for establishing your own class rules, or to review those already in place, or as a model for rules in other situations. Rules are a set of instructions for behaviour, and here they are expressed using *You should/must* which gives a less formal tone than the direct imperative that is common in instructional texts. The rules are expressed as positive instructions and could lead to discussing the effect of rules expressed as *Don't* or *You should not/must not*.

What's on the CD-ROM

The text on the CD-ROM is a writing frame that uses imperative verbs as sentence starters. Less able readers can engage in discussion about school rules and compose their own sets of rules in guided writing. They could also explore the effect of expressing rules in different ways, using *you* or as negatives.

Discussing the text

● Read the text, sharing understanding of ideas and vocabulary together. Compare them with rules already in place in your classroom, if appropriate. Discuss why rules are necessary (for example for safety, fairness and respect) and consider other familiar contexts in which rules are important.

● Consider each rule separately and discuss its reasons. Why is it important that children behave in this way? What would be the effect of not following the rule?

● Now look at the layout of the text, noting that each rule is a single sentence and each starts on a new line for clarity.

● Highlight *You* at the beginning of each sentence and talk about the effect of addressing the reader personally.

● Focus on the second word of each rule, discussing the effects of *should* and *must*. Establish that *must* is stronger and more definite, and *should* is perhaps more polite. Do children think that the *must* rules are more important? They should feel free to disagree

and should justify their opinion. They might feel that each rule should have the same word (either *must* or *should*).

● Take the opportunity to explore the irregular spelling of *should*, making connections to its family of *would* and *could*. Ask the children to practise the spellings on individual whiteboards.

● Cover *You must/should* and re-read the rules. Draw attention to the imperatives, which, now they are 'isolated', make the rules sound more direct and 'bossy'. Which version do the children prefer?

Talk, read and write

● In guided groups, model rephrasing the first rule as a negative (*You should not be rude or unkind to anyone*). Discuss the changes, noting *not* and the opposites (antonyms) of *polite* and *kind*. Ask children to consider other appropriate words, such as *cheeky, impolite* or *mean*. Then rephrase the rule further as a direct negative instruction (*Don't...* or *Do not...*). Children can then work in groups to rephrase other rules, discussing possible antonyms. Point out how the behaviour that is *not* wanted is now emphasised.

● Ask groups to discuss the relative importance of each rule. Each group should present and justify their decisions to the rest of the class.

● Use shared and independent writing to compose rules for your classroom or other familiar context, modelling positive phrasing. Ask the children to use response partners to check writing for sense and punctuation.

● In pairs or small groups ask the children to choose one rule and role play the possible consequences of not following it. Discuss the outcomes and the feelings of the characters involved (perhaps in circle time). Children could then role play and discuss the desired behaviour.

Extension

Ask children to talk to parents and carers about desirable rules at home and to write a list, expressed as *I should...* Less able writers could draw pictures. This could be used at the end of term as a starting point for New Year's resolutions.

2: 1: T18: to use appropriate register in writing instructions

2: 1: S4: to re-read own writing for sense and punctuation

rules are not given in any particular order; is there an order of importance?

imperative verbs qualified by 'should' and 'must' – makes tone slightly less 'bossy' than direct imperative

Classroom rules

You should always be polite and kind to everyone.

You should listen to other people when they have something to say.

You must put your hand up if you have something to say.

You should keep the classroom tidy.

You must always use equipment carefully.

You should work quietly and sensibly.

Text © 2007, Sue Taylor; pinboard photo © Davide Guglielmo

or 'You should not be rude or unkind to anyone'

addresses reader directly, makes personal connection

words that give advice; 'must' is stronger and more imperative than 'should'

2: 1: T13: to read simple written instructions in the classroom

2: 1: T15: to write simple instructions

2: 1: W9: to spell common irregular words from Appendix List 1

A Japanese Wishing Tree

by Sue Taylor

Background

The creation of a 'wishing tree' is inspired by a traditional Japanese story about the daughter of the sky god. She fell in love and no longer worked at weaving cloth for the gods. Her father stopped her crossing the river to where her young man lived. She was so sad that she still did no work. Her father relented and agreed that she could cross on one day each year. The people wished for good weather on that day because if it rained the river would be too deep to cross. They wrote their wishes on pieces of paper hung from a tree by the river. Japanese people continue the tradition of hanging their wishes for the future on a tree. This text gives instructions for making a wishing tree from paper. It could be used at the end of term as an alternative to New Year's resolutions.

What's on the CD-ROM

The text on the CD-ROM is a simpler version of the instructions in the core text. It provides greater visual support and gives the instructions in four steps, without background information.

Discussing the text

● Tell the story of the wishing tree, and perhaps locate Japan on a globe or map. Then ask the children to share with a partner one wish that they would put on a wishing tree. Share other experiences of making wishes (for example, when blowing out birthday candles).

● Read the title and ask the children to consider why *'grow'* is in inverted commas. (The text gives instructions for making a *paper* tree that does not really grow.) Note the capital letters in the title for names – of a nationality and a very particular tree.

● Read the text, identifying and establishing the purpose of structural features: title (the goal), background information (to set the scene and appeal to the reader), sequenced steps to achieve the goal, illustration (to aid understanding of the written text) and the template (as a model or example).

● Note how the first instruction directly addresses the reader, making the text seem very personal.

● Highlight the time connectives and discuss their role in reinforcing the sequence of steps. Explore the effect of re-ordering instructions,

noting that *First* and *Finally* absolutely identify a start and finish point, unlike *Then* and *Now.* Ask pairs of children to share other words for telling what order to do things in.

● Highlight *draw* and *cut* and elicit that they are the words that tell you what to do. Ask the children to find the other imperatives.

● Consider the impact of the layout of the list in leaf illustrations and the repetition of *one wish.*

● Now ask the children to recall whether the wish they thought of earlier was for themselves or someone else. Talk about the need to be careful with wishes because they might come true. (There are many traditional tales about 'wasted' or unkind wishes.)

● For word-level learning, highlight the 'ee' phonemes in *tree* and *leaf* and note the different diagraphs for spelling. Share other words with the 'ee' sound (*green* and *read* are also in the text) and categorise them into spelling patterns.

Talk, read and write

● As a class, share some ideas for the first type of wish – 'for myself'. Issues about the nature of wishes (for example material or abstract) can be discussed as they arise. Now ask the children to talk in pairs about the other kinds of wishes and then draft their five as sentences. Some children may need sentence starters, such as *For myself I wish for…* Ask response partners to check sentences for sense and punctuation before the children write on the leaves.

● Give the children enlarged copies of the text to label the key features identified in shared reading. These can be displayed alongside the wishing tree.

● Challenge the children to investigate other words with *ee* or *ea* spellings. These could also be displayed in tree and leaf shapes with the wishing tree.

Extension

Read a traditional tale about wasted wishes and use this as a starting point for children's own versions. For homework they could make notes or draw pictures of their ideas for a story.

2: 1: T14: to note key structural features, such as clear statement of purpose at start, sequential steps set out in a list, direct language

2: 1: S2: to find examples of words and phrases that link sentences

2: 1: S5: to revise knowledge about other uses of capitalisation

capital letters for name

background information sets scene

direct approach to reader; gives purpose to activity

shape to draw around

each subsequent wish is for a larger community; repetition of 'one wish' for impact

How to 'grow' a Japanese Wishing Tree

Make your wishes and hang them on the tree!
Japanese people hang their wishes on a special tree.
They believe that their wishes will come true when their leaves blow away.
Yours will stay on the tree for everyone to read.

First you will need to ask your teacher to help you draw the trunk and branches of a tree on a big display board.

I wish...

Then draw your leaf on light green paper and cut it out very carefully. You can use the template on the right.

Now write **five wishes** on your leaf, one from each little leaf:

one wish for yourself

one wish for your friends

one wish for your family

one wish for your school

one wish for the whole world

Finally hang your leaf on the tree. Use Blu-Tack or drawing pins.

Think carefully about your wishes before you write.

Text © 2007, Sue Taylor

2: 1: T13: to read simple written instructions

2: 1: W1: to secure identification, spelling and reading of long vowel digraphs in simple words

inverted commas because tree doesn't really grow as a live tree does

snappy, appealing tagline works well with picture

same sound, different digraph spelling

connectives that link sentences into a sequence

direct address to reader maintained throughout

...because they might come true!

2: 1: S4: to re-read own writing for sense and punctuation

Be safe with fireworks!

by Sue Taylor

Background

Fireworks are a topical subject in the autumn term. Many children will have attended firework displays or had fireworks at home and this context will therefore have meaning and relevance. The version of the firework code given in this text sets out seven key safety messages in direct imperative language. Some rules suggest do and some suggest don't giving the opportunity to explore differences in meaning and language structure. The picture engages attention by encouraging the reader to interact with the text. Unlike most of the other instructional texts explored (such as recipes and craft activities), these rules could be presented and followed in any order. This text can be linked to science and PSHE and to work in art and design exploring different media to create firework pictures.

What's on the CD-ROM

The differentiated version is a writing frame for the same text, with sentence starters to act as prompts. The same picture is included to encourage interaction and discussion. After sharing the core text, less able readers could use this frame to compose and then write their own sentences, perhaps using them as captions for pictures. All children will therefore be able to meet similar objectives.

Discussing the text

● Before showing the text, encourage the children to share their experiences of fireworks and what they know about the dangers and how to stay safe.

● Show the title, subtitle and illustration. Discuss the use of exclamation marks, and model reading aloud with appropriate expression. Note how the subheading appeals directly to the reader and invites him or her to interact with the text and make it his or her own.

● Allow the children to look carefully at the picture and work in pairs to see how many dangers they can spot. List these on the board.

● Now read the list of rules given in the text, and see how closely they match the dangers. Discuss the reasons for each rule.

● Point out that the rules are expressed as a set of instructions – some positive and some negative. Note that the positive instructions emphasise safe behaviour and the negative ones focus on danger.

● Highlight *Keep* and *Store* and elicit their function as the 'bossy' words that tell you what to do. Ask children to highlight the other imperatives, noting that in the *Don't* rule the imperative is the second word in the sentence because the negative has to come first. Note also the emphasis created by *Never* and *Always*, and that they are opposites.

● Talk about the reader-friendly impact of the layout as a list, with each rule on a new line and a single short sentence. Consider whether the order of the rules matters, relating this to other instructional texts studied where there is a definite sequence (although children might have views about the order of importance).

● Take the opportunity to reinforce reading and spelling of high frequency words that occur in the text, perhaps using individual whiteboards and strategies such as Look-Say-Cover-Write-Check. Develop this with games such as matching pairs or have 'speed spelling' competitions.

Talk, read and write

● Organise small groups and allocate a rule to each for the children to illustrate through role play. They could represent first the danger and then the safe action.

● Then ask the groups to illustrate their rule, with a picture and caption expressed in direct language. These could be displayed around the school. Less able writers could do labelled pictures and more able writers could suggest their own rules. Alternatively, this could be developed into book-making, with groups making a book of rules for other classes.

Extension

Choose another familiar context and ask children to draw 'spot the danger' pictures. This can then be developed using shared, guided and independent writing to compose safety rules. You might also use role play again to develop talk for writing.

Ask children to explore the effect of expressing these rules as *Do...* or *Don't...* Encourage children to work with response partners to check and edit their sentences.

2: 1: T17: to use diagrams in instructions

2: 1: W9: to spell common irregular words from Appendix List 1

exclamation marks draw attention and add emphasis

emphasise the importance of these rules – one negative ('Don't'), one positive ('Do')

in case it explodes suddenly or shoots out sparks

in case the sparks burn or the sparkler burns down

2: 1: S4: to re-read own writing for sense and punctuation

Be safe with fireworks!

Spot the danger!

Text © 2007, Sue Taylor; firework photo © Jason Britton; illustration © Baz Rowell/Beehive Illustration

Follow the rules

* Always let an adult light fireworks.
* Stand well back when a firework has been lit.
* Wear gloves to hold sparklers.

* Keep all your pets indoors.
* Store your fireworks in a closed tin.
* Never play with fireworks.
* Don't put fireworks in your pockets.

title is an instruction itself

subheading is also an instruction; introduces the picture

2: 1: T13: to read simple written instructions in the classroom

2: 1: T18: to use appropriate register in writing instructions

picture shows what not to do; immediately draws in reader to interact with text

each rule acts as a 'Do' or 'Don't'; short, simple sentences that can be read and understood quickly and remembered

they might be frightened or get hurt

here the main verb works with 'Don't' to make a negative imperative

2: 1: S3: to recognise and take account of exclamation marks

Making dummy fireworks by Jill Bennett and Archie Millar

Background

This extract would work well in conjunction with the previous text on firework safety. It has cross-curricular links with maths (3D shapes) and design and technology. The text itself is from a teacher resource book, so the intended reader is the teacher, not the children. It offers the opportunity to explore ways in which language varies according to audience. Children could rewrite the extract as a set of instructions for children, and then present them to other classes in the school. This will give a purpose for focusing closely on the structure and language of instructional texts. This text is likely to be most effective if used after other, more conventional, instructional texts have been studied and their key features identified.

What's on the CD-ROM

The differentiated text is a set of instructions for making dummy fireworks, written for children. It is written in simple language that addresses the child directly, so makes an interesting comparison with the core text. For less able readers it offers a straightforward opportunity to explore key features of instructional texts, including the list of materials needed and numbered sequential steps. After children have made the fireworks, this text could be used in guided reading and writing to sequence the instructions.

Discussing the text

● Read the text with the children and ask for observations. What is the text about? Who is it for? Where does it come from? Draw out the fact that it is from a resource book for a teacher and gives instructions and suggestions for making fireworks with the children in his or her class. Clarify any difficult vocabulary.

● Read the text again, stopping at each section to identify the features that suggest a teacher is the intended reader. For example: the number *1* in the title suggests that there is a companion text, and indicates that it comes from a book, as does *see page 120*; *Age range* and *Group size* and the first paragraph of *What to do* tells the teacher what to tell the children and the second paragraph gives further ideas for the classroom.

● Remind the children of other instructional texts studied. Recap and list key features, such as the goal, materials needed, sequence of steps to achieve goal, use of direct language (including imperatives), numbers or bullet points and connectives to link steps in chronological order.

● Ask the children to identify any of these features in this text and note which are not used.

Talk, read and write

● Children can now make the fireworks as you 'think aloud' through each step of the text to demonstrate how you are using the guidance and instructions. You could tell the class afterwards how effective the instructions were for you as a teacher.

● Explain that they are now going to write a set of instructions to tell other children how to make the fireworks.

● First draw up a list together, in note form, of the steps they needed to complete their dummy fireworks. Using these notes and the genre features identified earlier, model how to draw up a set of instructions. Again, think aloud at each step, involving the children in decisions about which aspects are to be included and the structural and language features used. Re-read the text frequently to ensure that the language is appropriate for the audience and to check for sense and completeness.

● Now ask the children to use this model to write sets of instructions to take to other classes (with examples of fireworks made). Encourage them to add diagrams to help other children to understand the instructions. They might also consider whether any other information would be valuable, such as introductory or closing sentences to appeal to the readers and make them want to read on and try out the instructions.

Extension

In class, share words and phrases associated with fireworks, drawing on colours, shapes, sounds, smells and emotions. Then, for homework, children could use these to write acrostics as suggested in the text. Some children might extend the words and phrases into sentences to create longer lines of poetry.

2: 1: T16: to use models from reading to organise instructions sequentially

2: 1: T18: to use appropriate register in writing instructions

2: 1: S4: to re-read own writing for sense and punctuation

confirms text is for teacher

indicates there is a second text

indicates text is taken from a book

'not real' ie, not groups

Making dummy fireworks ①

Age range
Seven to nine

Group size
Individuals

What you need
Copies of nets for pyramids (see page 120) cardboard tubes, felt-tipped pens, scissors, adhesive

What to do
First discuss the names of the various 3D shapes with the children. They can then make dummy fireworks using the copies of the nets and the cardboard cylinders. Cut out the nets and then decorate them with felt-tipped pens (this should be done before the shapes are stuck). Make sure the children make their design so that any writing will be the right way up when the shape is stuck together. Ask the children to make up exotic names for their fireworks.

The finished shapes can be displayed against a 'fire' painting and the firework code cartoons. Alternatively a background of acrostic words built up on the word 'fireworks' could be used as a background. These words could illustrate the sights, sounds and atmosphere of a firework display.

Text extract from
"Bright Ideas: Festivals" by Jill Bennett and Archie Millar © 1988, Jill Bennett and Archie Millar © 1988 Scholastic Ltd); illustration © Ray & Corinne Burrows/Beehive Illustration

tip for successful outcome

poem in which the first letters of the lines form the word ('fireworks')

2nd paragraph gives suggestions for display

unusual, exciting, mysterious

additional information given in brackets

instructions for teacher; set out in prose paragraph, not list

glue

template for making shape

subheadings: advice for teacher

2: 1: T15: to write simple instructions

2: 1: T17: to use diagrams in instructions

2: 1: W10: to learn new words from reading linked to particular topics

Whale — which

from *Collins Junior Dictionary*

Background

This extract from the *Collins Junior Dictionary* has many features typical of dictionaries. Headwords and other related words are clearly identified and entries indicate the word class. Grammatical terminology can be discussed at an appropriate level, but it is less important for children to understand the terms than to know what information is included in a dictionary. The guide word works as a heading to assist the reader to locate words, and the alphabet is included for reference. Most entries include a sentence incorporating the headword to demonstrate its use. It is notable that where words are nouns a definition is possible, but other word classes can only be described in terms of their function. The extract contains words beginning with *wh* to reinforce reading and spelling of this digraph and also of high frequency words, particularly those used to form questions.

What's on the CD-ROM

This is a similar dictionary extract. There are fewer entries and less additional information. Some entries are supported by pictures. This will allow less able readers to explore the purpose of dictionaries for spelling and meanings with fewer reading demands. As in the core text, it contains words beginning with *wh* so that the same spelling and vocabulary objectives can be met.

Discussing the text

● Show the text and ask the children where they think it came from. Present a range of dictionaries and share understanding of the twofold purpose of dictionaries – for spellings and meanings.

● Highlight the guide word at the top of the page and explain its function in assisting the reader to locate particular words. Look at other dictionaries to explore other presentation methods.

● Note the alphabet down the side of the page, reinforcing the alphabetical nature of dictionaries. Draw attention to the highlighted *Ww* that pinpoints the entries on this page. Recite the alphabet to reinforce ordering.

● Highlight the headwords and ask the children what they notice about their spelling

(they all begin with *wh*). Read them together and note that the *h* is silent. Children might be able to identify how the entries have been ordered, by second, third and fourth letter.

● Use different colours to highlight the two parts of *wheelbarrow* and *wheelchair* to establish the meaning of each part and the whole. Note that splitting them can help with reading and spelling. Discuss other compounds.

● Focus on the first entry and identify each feature. Read the definition and ask the children to share their own knowledge of whales.

● Now read and explore features of the second entry, noting that this time the word is put into a sentence to demonstrate its meaning and use.

● After discussing other entries, highlight and list all the *wh* question words from the text. Share other question words and practise their spellings.

Talk, read and write

● Give the children sets of words to order alphabetically, by first, second or third letter as appropriate.

● Demonstrate how to use quartiles to find words quickly, using large cards to show the divisions (*abcdefg*, *hijklmn*, *opqrst*, *uvwxyz*). Say or write some words and ask the children to hold up the right number of fingers to indicate the quartile. Challenge the class to find words in dictionaries as quickly as possible.

● Model how to write definitions of simple nouns (which might be related to a current topic). Children could then write their own definitions and challenge others to guess their words.

● Practise reading and spelling of *wh* question words, for example by putting them in a wordsearch.

● Ask the children to suggest other compound words and illustrate their meanings as two parts and as a whole. Some children may benefit from having words on cards to put together.

Extension

Ask children to make 'Guess what I am' books. They should choose a familiar noun and write a definition to challenge others. They can then reveal the word (on the next page or under a flap). Give some children simple definitions to illustrate and present in the same format.

2: 2: T17: to know that dictionaries and glossaries give definitions and explanations

type of animal – same group as humans; a whale isn't a fish

additional information about creature (mammals breathe air)

compound words

headwords in bold

two ways of using word

...so, 'I don't know if I can go'

pronounced 'w' in all these examples – 'h' is silent

definition

2: 2: S7: to investigate and recognise a range of other ways of presenting texts

Whale

a
b **whale** whales
NOUN A **whale** is a huge mammal that lives in the sea. Whales breathe through an opening in the top of their head.
c
d
e
f
g
h **what**
ADJECTIVE OR PRONOUN **1 What** is used in questions. *What time is it? What is your name?*
PRONOUN **2** You can use **what** to refer to information about something. *I don't know what you mean.*
What about PHRASE You say what **about** at the beginning of a question when you are making a suggestion or offer. *What about a sandwich?*
i
j
k
l
m
n
o
p
q
r
s
t **wheat**
NOUN **Wheat** is a cereal plant grown for its grain, which is used to make flour.
u
v **wheel** wheels
NOUN A **wheel** is a circular object which turns round on a rod fixed to its centre. Wheels are fitted under things such as cars, bicycles and prams so that they can move along.
Ww
x
y
z

wheelbarrow wheelbarrows
NOUN A **wheelbarrow** is a small cart with a single wheel at the front.

wheelchair wheelchairs
NOUN A **wheelchair** is a chair with large wheels for use by people who find walking difficult or impossible.

when
ADVERB **1** You use **when** to ask what time something happened or will happen. *When are you leaving?*
CONJUNCTION **2** You use **when** to refer to a certain time. *I met him when we were at school together.*

where
ADVERB **1** You use **where** to ask questions about place. *Where is my book?*
CONJUNCTION **2** You use **where** to talk about the place in which something is situated or happening. *I don't know where we are.*

whether
CONJUNCTION You can use **whether** instead of **if**. *I don't know whether I can go.*

which
ADJECTIVE **1** You use **which** to ask for information about something when there are two or more possibilities. *Which room are you in?*
PRONOUN **2** You also use **which** when you are going to say more about something you have already mentioned. *We have a car which is dropping to bits.*

Text extract from "Collins Junior Dictionary", compiled by Evelyn Goldsmith © 2000, Harper Collins Publishers Ltd (2000, Collins); photos: whale © Keran McKenzie wheat © Frank Van Den Berg, wheel, wheel © Helmut Gevert, wheelbarrow © Davide Guglielmo

2: 2: T16: to use dictionaries and glossaries to locate words by using initial letter

guide word shows first entry on page

2: 2: W3: to read and spell words containing the diagraph 'wh'

additional forms – in this case, plural; plural also used in definition

examples of use within sentences, or questions, given in italic

specific phrase with a different way of using main word

nouns have simple definitions

highlight within alphabetical list shows focus of this page; marginal list reinforces alphabetical nature of dictionary

word class in small caps

2: 2: W4: to split familiar oral and written compound words into their component parts

Science dictionary 'ad — bl' from *Science Dictionary*

Background
This extract from a scientific dictionary demonstrates many key features and presentational techniques of such alphabetic texts. It shows the range of words that can be found on each page (using second-letter alphabetical order) and gives simple definitions. Many of the terms will be familiar to children through general knowledge and topics studied in science, but other vocabulary might well be unfamiliar. Pictures aid understanding of the definitions and in some cases provide additional information and vocabulary. The text provides a simple starting point for a subject-specific dictionary, used for a particular purpose. It might be used in conjunction with the text 'The life cycle of a frog' on page 62.

What's on the CD-ROM
This is a similar dictionary page. The text lists just five words and their definitions, each headword beginning with a different letter of the alphabet, so that only first-letter alphabetical order is needed. The alphabet is listed at the side of the page to reinforce understanding of alphabetical order, and every entry is illustrated. The text demonstrates the same key features of the core text to enable less able readers to meet similar objectives for working with alphabetically ordered texts.

Discussing the text
● If possible, have a range of dictionaries on display, particularly those that are subject-specific, such as for geography and maths.
● Read the text and ask where it might have come from, prompting where necessary by pointing out typical features. After establishing the text type, focus on the headwords to help the children to see they are all related to science topics. Discuss who might use this dictionary and why.
● Ask the children what letters the words begin with, and elicit that this page must be from the beginning of the dictionary. Recite or sing the alphabet. Ask the children why the words are in the order they are to prompt them to identify ordering by second or third letter.
● Highlight significant visual features on the page: guide letters at the top, bold and italic type, bullet points (as points and as arrows),

pictures and labels – and consider their different purposes and effects.
● Read each definition in turn and clarify the meanings. Model strategies for reading unfamiliar words. Note that the definitions are not written in complete sentences, but there is enough for understanding. Model how one or two can be made into sentences, for example *An amphibian is…* A different model is needed for the adjective *blind*, such as *Someone who is blind cannot see.*
● Focus on the arrow bullets and explain that these direct the reader to other related entries that provide additional information about this word. Note that the entry for *bean* lists two additional words, separated by a comma.
● Discuss how the pictures aid understanding of the definitions and sometimes give additional information. Consider whether illustrations are provided for the most 'difficult' entries. Would diagrams assist their understanding of other entries?

Talk, read and write
● Give the children words relating to a relevant science topic to put into alphabetical order. This can be differentiated by giving sets of words that require first-, second- or third-letter ordering. Some children might need labelled pictures to sequence.
● In shared writing, model the composition of definitions for some other current topic words. Then ask the children to work in pairs to write definitions for other words. Some might need to match words to prepared definitions. The words can then be arranged into alphabetical order for a class topic dictionary.
● Give groups a range of dictionaries to explore. Ask them to consider their purpose and evaluate their ease of use, organising this into a presentation to the class.
● Say or write pairs of words and ask the children which would come first in the dictionary. Then challenge the children to find words in dictionaries as quickly as possible. This can be differentiated by the dictionary used.

Extension
Ask children to write a list of things in their bedrooms in alphabetical order. Encourage more able learners to write definitions as well.

2: 2: T20: to make class dictionaries and glossaries of special interest words, giving explanations and definitions

pictures aid understanding; labels and arrows demonstrate a process

only entry here that is not a noun – an adjective

2: 2: S7: to investigate and recognise a range of other ways of presenting texts

shows the beginnings of the first and last words on these pages ('adult' and 'arm'; and 'baby' and 'blossom') requires 2nd letter alphabetical order

headwords

prefix 'un', meaning 'not'

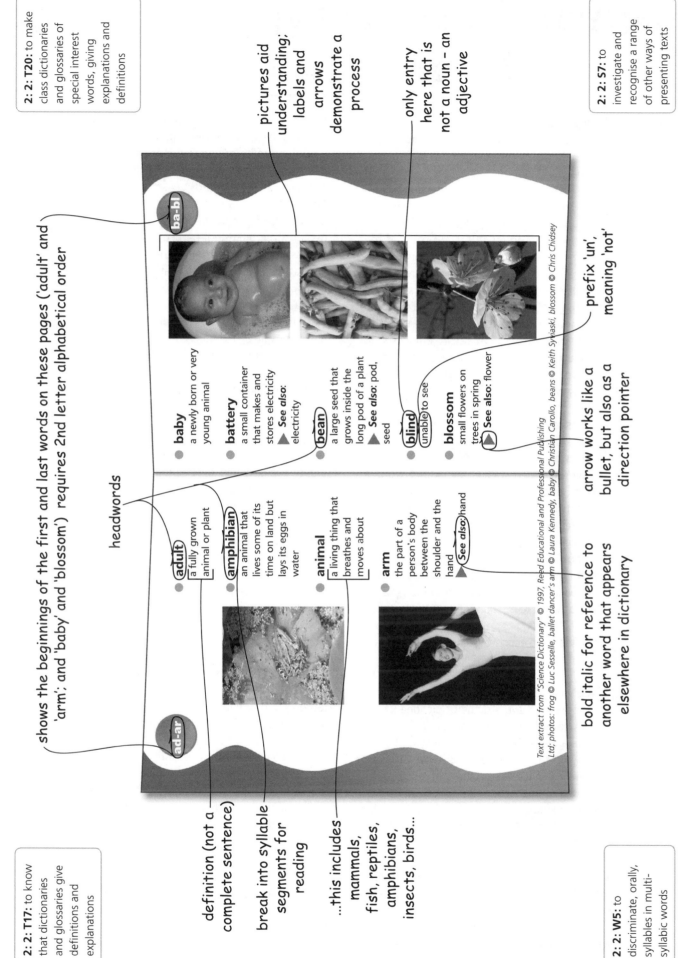

ba-bl

baby
a newly born or very young animal

battery
a small container that makes and stores electricity
▲ *See also:* electricity

bean
a large seed that grows inside the long pod of a plant
▲ *See also:* pod, seed

blind
unable to see

blossom
small flowers on trees in spring
▲ *See also:* flower

ad-ar

adult
a fully grown animal or plant

amphibian
an animal that lives some of its time on land but lays its eggs in water

animal
a living thing that breathes and moves about

arm
the part of a person's body between the shoulder and the hand
▲ *See also:* hand

Text extract from "Science Dictionary" © 1997, Reed Educational and Professional Publishing Ltd; photos: frog © Luc Sesselle, ballet dancer's arm © Laura Kennedy; baby © Christian Carollo, beans © Keith Sylvaski, blossom © Chris Chidsey

arrow works like a bullet, but also as a direction pointer

bold italic for reference to another word that appears elsewhere in dictionary

2: 2: T17: to know that dictionaries and glossaries give definitions and explanations

definition (not a complete sentence)

break into syllable segments for reading

...this includes mammals, fish, reptiles, amphibians, insects, birds...

2: 2: W5: to discriminate, orally, syllables in multi-syllabic words

Maths dictionary '-teen'
by Scholastic Ltd

Background

This extract continues children's understanding of the purpose and use of subject-specific dictionaries. It is particularly useful when used in conjunction with the previous extract from a science dictionary. The text contains definitions, explanations and examples of some key mathematical concepts. Although some of the terms might not yet have been encountered by Year 2 children, the explanations are simple enough to allow at least some understanding. Other concepts will be familiar and will reinforce key vocabulary. The text uses underlining to indicate terminology that occurs elsewhere in the dictionary. Some entries are supported by illustrations with captions that demonstrate the vocabulary in use. The text should, if possible, be used in conjunction with other dictionaries, and ideally other special-purpose ones.

What's on the CD-ROM

The differentiated text is an extract from a simpler maths dictionary. Explanations are briefer, use more basic language and each is supported by illustrations. The alphabet is listed at the side of the page to reinforce alphabetical ordering. The concepts themselves are similar to that in the core text to give less able readers the opportunity to engage with the vocabulary in similar ways to others. The text can be used in guided reading to explore the purpose and use of a subject-specific dictionary at an appropriate reading level.

Discussing the text

● If possible, have a range of dictionaries on display, including subject-specific ones. Show the text and ask the children what kind of book they think it is taken from, and how they can tell. Share previous experiences of dictionaries, establishing that they are used to check spellings of words and give meanings. Read the list of headwords (pointing out that these are in bold) and elicit that they are all words related to numbers and, therefore, to maths.

● Highlight the heading/guide word, noting that this shows the first entry on the page and helps the reader to find particular words in the dictionary. Focus on the headwords again and consider their order, establishing the need for first-, second- and third-letter ordering.

● Read each entry, explaining unfamiliar terminology and concepts at an appropriate level. Note that a maths dictionary is, by its very nature, full of technical terms. Children might notice that some words, such as *third* and *times*, have other meanings. Explore the pictures and captions and note how they demonstrate the use of particular words.

● Ask the children why they think some words are underlined. Elicit that they are also to be found in the dictionary, so the reader can look up further definitions and explanations. Note that sometimes the reader is referred to another entry for the actual explanation (*See...*), where there is an alternative term.

Talk, read and write

● Take words from a current maths topic and use shared writing to model the composition of simple definitions and explanations. Add illustrations and sentence captions as in the text where these would be helpful. Then ask the children to write their own definitions of relevant words. Encourage some children to add cross-references to other entries where appropriate. To support others, provide given definitions or illustrations to words for matching, or work together in guided writing. The words and definitions can then be compiled into alphabetically ordered, illustrated, personal or class dictionaries for the topic, or used for display in the maths area.

● To reinforce alphabetical order, give the children sets of words from a current topic to order alphabetically – by first, second or third letter as appropriate.

● Give the children a range of dictionaries, both general and subject-specific and ask them to consider their purpose and evaluate their ease of use.

● Challenge pairs of children to find words in dictionaries as quickly as possible. This can be differentiated by the dictionary given and the words chosen.

Extension

For homework, ask children to write definitions for appropriate maths vocabulary for others to guess the words. Encourage children to practise reading and spelling vocabulary from a current maths topic.

2: 2: T18: to use other alphabetically ordered texts

underlined words can also be found in this dictionary

similar explanation to that for 'ten'

2: 2: T20: to make class dictionaries and glossaries of special interest words, giving explanations and definitions

-teen

-teen A suffix that means a number from 13 to 19.

ten A whole number made up of ten ones, or units. It is written as 10. Multiples of ten include numbers ending in 0, such as 20, 30, 40 and 50. Something that is split into ten equal parts is made up of ten tenths.

third This is not a whole number, it is a fraction. A third is one of three equal parts that make up a whole.

thousand A whole number made up of ten hundreds. It is written as 1000. Something that is split into one thousand equal parts is made up of a thousand thousandths.

times Another way of saying multiplied by.

times-tables These are lists of whole numbers multiplied by other numbers. For example, the two times table starts as follows:

$1 \times 2 = 2$
$2 \times 2 = 4$
$3 \times 2 = 6$
$4 \times 2 = 8$
$5 \times 2 = 10$
$6 \times 2 = 12$
and so on.

total The result of adding a groups of numbers together – how much they make altogether.

▲ Each **third** of this flag is a different colour.

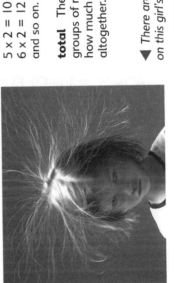

▼ There are **thousands** of hairs on this girl's head.

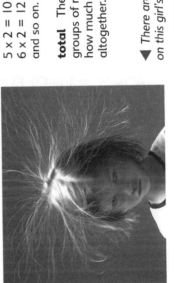

Text © 2007, Scholastic Ltd; photos: hair © Darrell Coomes, flag © Vuillioud Piere Andre

identifies first word defined on this page

numbers that end in '-teen'

puts the word into a sentence to illustrate its meaning

also an ordinal number

headwords in bold

3rd-letter ordering

2: 2: T17: to know that dictionaries and glossaries give definitions and explanations

2: 2: S7: to investigate and recognise a range of other ways of presenting text

Rhyming dictionary

by John Foster

Background

This extract is from a rhyming dictionary that can be used to find families of rhyming words, perhaps for poetry writing, and to support spelling. The dictionary is organised in alphabetical order based on the most common words in each rhyming family. Each entry identifies the rhyming sound and lists, in alphabetical order and collected by the same spelling pattern (rime), words with the same sound. The text is supported by an illustration and includes a short poem that incorporates words in the rhyming family. The text can be used alongside others to illustrate the range of different dictionaries. This particular extract is for the key word *shore* and can therefore be used to support reading and spelling of the vowel phoneme 'or'.

What's on the CD-ROM

This is another extract from the same dictionary, based on the key word *tail*, with the alternative rime *-ale*, which will provide opportunities to revise reading and spelling of the long vowel phoneme 'ai'. There is a short, illustrated rhyme incorporating words with both spelling patterns to demonstrate them in use. With only two alternative rimes, the text will be more accessible to less able readers and spellers and can be used in guided sessions to explore the two spelling families and word meanings.

Discussing the text

● Read the first few lines of the text and ask children what they notice about the words. Repeat the words together, having fun with the sounds. Explain that this is an extract from a special kind of dictionary. Note the alphabet down the side of the page with *s* highlighted, reminding the reader of the alphabetical organisation of dictionaries.

● Read the first family of words again (*-ore*), checking understanding where necessary. Highlight the rime of each word (the common spelling pattern that makes the rhyming sound), noting that they are all the same. Emphasise that these words sound the same *and* have the same spelling pattern. Highlight the onsets (the opening part of the word) in a different colour (or first syllable in the case of *explore*) to show that the words are listed in alphabetical order.

● Read the next set of words (*-oar*). Elicit that they rhyme with the first set but have a different spelling pattern. Note that *oar* has no onset.

● Repeat with *-aw* words, which is quite a large family, and the *Other words that rhyme with shore*. Children by this stage will be aware that there are a lot of different ways of spelling the same sound and that choices have to be made when spelling. Encourage children to use dictionaries only after they have tried to spell a word using known spelling patterns.

● Read the poem with the children and ask them to highlight all the words with the 'or' phoneme. List these in their spelling families. Discuss the effect of *ROAR!* in large, bold capitals with the exclamation mark.

Talk, read and write

● Give the children onsets and rimes, from the words in the text, to match. Encourage them to illustrate the words or put them into sentences to demonstrate understanding. Some children might be able to generate further words in the family. Point out the homophones that occur, such as *saw/sore/soar* and *bore/boar*.

● In shared or guided writing, write a new verse for the *Dinah Shore* poem, using the same repeating structure and composing new lines based on the rhyming family. Ensure the children experiment orally with words and sounds before writing. They could then write more verses independently and illustrate them for display.

● Choose a different rhyming family (such as 'air') and use the alphabet to find onsets and generate words (including digraphs or blends if appropriate). This should be done orally initially, and children will need to decide whether they have made a real word. Discuss the common spelling patterns of the phoneme (*-air, -are, -ear, -ere*) and use dictionaries to categorise them. Encourage the children to write new poems based on the rhyming family.

Extension

Ask children to generate as many words as they can from a given rhyme. These could be used to make sentences that include as many of the words as possible. Set a challenge for the longest (and/or silliest!) sentence.

2: 2: T18: to use other alphabetically ordered texts

poem shows rhymes 'in action'

caps and bold for effect

2: 2: S7: to investigate and recognise a range of other ways of presenting texts

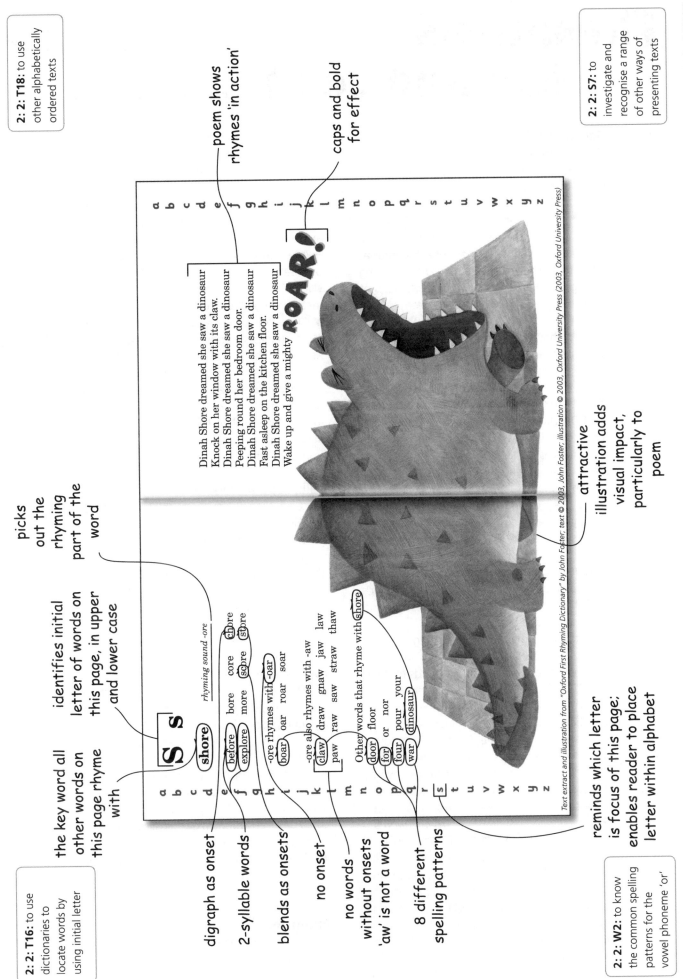

a
b
c
d
e
f
g
h
i
j
k
l
m
n
o
p
q
r
s
t
u
v
w
x
y
z

Dinah Shore dreamed she saw a dinosaur
Knock on her window with its claw.
Dinah Shore dreamed she saw a dinosaur
Peeping round her bedroom door.
Dinah Shore dreamed she saw a dinosaur
Fast asleep on the kitchen floor.
Dinah Shore dreamed she saw a dinosaur
Wake up and give a mighty **ROAR!**

attractive illustration adds visual impact, particularly to poem

Text extract and illustration from "Oxford First Rhyming Dictionary" by John Foster; text © 2003, John Foster; Illustration © 2003, Oxford University Press (2003, Oxford University Press)

picks out the rhyming part of the word

the key word all other words on this page rhyme with

identifies initial letter of words on this page, in upper and lower case

S s

shore   *rhyming sound -ore*

a
b
c
d   before   bore   core   chore
e   explore   more   score
f
g   -ore rhymes with -oar
h   boar   oar   roar   soar
i
j   -ore also rhymes with -aw
k   claw   draw   gnaw   jaw   law
l   paw   raw   saw   straw   thaw
m
n   Other words that rhyme with shore
o   door   floor
p   for   or   nor
q   four   pour   your
r   war   dinosaur
s
t
u
v
w
x
y
z

digraph as onset

2-syllable words

blends as onsets

no onset

no words without onsets 'aw' is not a word

8 different spelling patterns

reminds which letter is focus of this page; enables reader to place letter within alphabet

2: 2: T16: to use dictionaries to locate words by using initial letter

2: 2: W2: to know the common spelling patterns for the vowel phoneme 'or'

Thesaurus — bad and good by Andrew Delahunty

Background

These extracts introduce another type of alphabetically ordered text. The text suggests a range of synonyms for two words commonly overused in children's writing. The words are placed in sentences to suggest shades of meaning and choices in different contexts. Children will learn the purpose of a thesaurus as a tool for developing vocabulary and improving writing. The text also allows the exploration of antonyms. These two words have been selected to allow discussion of particular meanings, but children should be aware that they would not normally be found together in an alphabetically ordered thesaurus.

What's on the CD-ROM

The CD-ROM offers the same text in a simplified form. Synonyms for *bad* and *good* are offered in sentences to demonstrate their use and effect. The sentences can be used in guided writing as models for children's own sentences, where they can suggest further alternatives. Antonyms can also be explored so less able readers will be able to meet similar objectives.

Discussing the text

● If possible, display a range of dictionaries and thesauruses, revising the purpose and organisation of a dictionary.

● Introduce the text, explaining that it consists of *extracts* from a *thesaurus*, which can help them find more interesting words for their writing, as suggested by *Find a better word!*

● Explain that a thesaurus is organised in alphabetical order, like a dictionary.

● Note the bold type for the headwords, which helps the reader to find particular words. Read the introductory sentences for *bad*, which reinforce the purpose of a thesaurus. Stress that a thesaurus does not give *definitions* of words like a dictionary; it suggests *alternative* words.

● Read the first sentence and the alternative suggested. Substitute the alternative into the sentence and evaluate the effect, comparing the meanings of *naughty* and *bad*. Ask the children to suggest other possibilities, discussing their specific meanings. Note how they suggest particular types of 'badness' and, therefore, give a more precise description than *bad*. Introduce the word *synonym* to indicate words

with *similar* meanings, and explain how a writer chooses a particular word to convey a particular meaning. Repeat for other sentences.

● Note that *nice* is also an overused word and is not very precise in its meaning, and consider further alternatives in these examples. For example, *a **good** king* might be *fair, friendly, helpful, clever, sensible…*; *a **good** smell* could be *delicious, tasty, delightful, appetising. Wicked* might generate debate – today it can mean both bad and good.

● Focus on opposites, noting that a thesaurus often suggests opposites as well as words of similar meaning. Introduce the term *antonym* (comparing similarities of sound and spelling with *synonym*). Give the children other adjectives such as *big* or *loud* and ask them to suggest their antonyms. Note that some opposites are made by adding *un-* or *dis-* to words (using *kind* from the text as an example).

Talk, read and write

● Give the children a short text with *bad* and/or *good* repeated. Ask them to substitute synonyms, and then compare the effect. They could use the core text examples or their own choices. The texts can be differentiated according to ability, and the activity can be done orally. This activity could also be done using a word processor's thesaurus. Ensure the children evaluate the alternative options in order to select the word that most effectively conveys a particular meaning.

● Discuss other overused words (such as *said*). Generate alternatives using thesauruses as appropriate. Then ask the children to role play sentences with different synonyms to demonstrate precision and effect.

● Give the children words to find antonyms for. Allow them to use dictionaries and thesauruses, if appropriate. Some children could be given antonym pairs to illustrate. More able learners could use them in sentences.

● Create an alphabetically ordered class thesaurus of common words, with examples of their use.

Extension

Ask children to make posters of alternatives for commonly used words, to act as prompts for writing.

2: 2: W8: to spell words with common prefixes

depends on reader's feelings – someone else might say 'exciting'

antonym is made with the prefix 'un'

an overused word

2: 2: S9: to secure the use of simple sentences in own writing

technical term for a particular type of reference text

...but similar

'used very often'

new headword

encourages reader and tells purpose of thesaurus

the two words on this page are antonyms of each other

good

Good is a very common word and it has a lot of different meanings.
You can often use another word instead.

This is a good book.
You could say **enjoyable** instead.

Be a good boy.
You could say **well-behaved** instead.

He was a good king.
You could say **kind** or **nice** instead.

There's a good smell coming from the oven.
You could say **nice** or **lovely** or **fine** instead.

This work is good.
You could say **well done** instead.

The opposite of good is bad.

a b c d e f g h i j k l m n o p q r s t u v w x y z

Thesaurus
Find a better word!

bad

Bad is a very common word and it has a lot of different meanings.
You can often use another word instead.

What a bad child!
You could say **naughty** instead.

The king was a bad man.
You could say **wicked** instead.

She is bad at spelling.
You could say **poor** instead.

There's a bad smell coming from the dustbin.
You could say **nasty** or **revolting** or **horrible** instead.

I feel bad about forgetting his birthday.
You could say **awful** or **dreadful** or **terrible** instead.

The opposite of bad is good.

a b c d e f g h i j k l m n o p q r s t u v w x y z

Text extracts from "Oxford First Thesaurus" by Andrew Delahunty © 2002, Andrew Delahunty (2002, Oxford University Press); Photos © 2006, Jupiter Images

headword

...to make writing more interesting and more precise

example sentences containing headword given in italic

also called 'antonym'; an antonym 'reverses' the meaning

suggestions for synonyms given in bold; synonyms have similar meanings – not all will will fit every sentence, depending on meaning; each sentence needs to be read with alternative to assess sense and effect

2: 2: T18: to use other alphabetically ordered texts

2: 2: W10: to learn new words from reading

2: 2: W11: to learn the use of antonyms

Class 2 directory

by Sue Taylor

Background

Directories are a form of alphabetically ordered text that children will need to use in everyday life. Telephone directories are likely to be challenging for this age group, so this extract provides an accessible introduction to such texts. It lists the children in an imaginary Year 2 class and includes full addresses and telephone numbers. The text provides the opportunity for children to learn to read and write their own addresses. It might be linked to a topic on local geography, for example exploring road names. It could also be used in conjunction with 'Journey of a letter' on page 70.

What's on the CD-ROM

The simplified version on the CD-ROM contains fewer entries and only one name beginning with any letter of the alphabet, so that children can focus on alphabetical order by first letter. It contains the same personal details, so that all children have the opportunity to explore the text features and meet the same objectives.

Discussing the text

● Show the title and talk about the term *directory*. Show the children a range of directories and ask if they recognise them and know when and why they are used.

● Show the rest of the text and read the first two entries. Consider each piece of information, relating it to the children's own details to ensure understanding. Discuss the importance of knowing one's own address and telephone number. You might also talk about the form and styles of email addresses.

● Relating each point to the children themselves, talk about why the surname comes first. (The *family* name is considered to be more important and identifiable in formal contexts.) What is the letter after the surname? What does each part of the address indicate? Why does the telephone number have two parts and why is the first part always the same?

● Read other entries to see different types of address, such as flat numbers and houses that have names rather than numbers.

● Highlight different words for types of road – *Drive, Street, Avenue...* Compare these with street names that the children know from experience. Consider what kind of road they think each name suggests (for example, a wide avenue, an enclosed drive).

● Highlight the postcodes, explaining the function of each part as in the annotations. Discuss the value of postcodes in sorting mail quickly. Relate them to other familiar abbreviations or shorthands such as *Mr, Dr* and perhaps bar codes and text messages.

● Consider features of text presentation. Why are the names in alphabetical order? Note the bold capitals that further help the surname to stand out, and draw attention to the initial capital letter for every name in the address.

● Highlight the commas to identify each part of the address. Rewrite the first entry as it would appear on an envelope to demonstrate that commas indicate a new line.

Talk, read and write

● Help the children to write their own names and addresses. Some might know these already; some might need to be given a copy. If possible, ask the children to write their name and address on an envelope (for a newsletter to be sent home for example). They could then write it as it would appear in a directory, using the model in the text.

● Give the children cut-up copies of the text, or similar list of your own class, to re-order alphabetically. Alternatively, give children an individual entry to re-order correctly.

● Practise alphabetical ordering, using names of children in the class and/or teachers in the school. This can be differentiated by first-, second- or third-letter order.

● In guided reading, help the children to investigate a range of directories to establish purposes and compare organisation and layouts, for example business or residential listings, classified directories.

● As part of a topic on local geography, investigate the origins of names of streets or buildings. You might also explore 'Journey of a letter' using the text on page 70.

Extension

For homework, ask children to practise writing their name and address. They could also learn to write the school's name and address.

Ask children to write a letter to a story character, making up an appropriate address.

2: 2: **W6:** to read on sight and spell all the words from Appendix List 1

2: 2: **S8:** to use commas to separate items in a list

CLASS 2 DIRECTORY OF ADDRESSES AND TELEPHONE NUMBERS

ABBOTT, R,	6 West Drive, Hinton, Essex, AT12 3JG	(01231) 345986
ADAMS, J,	17 New Street, Hinton, Essex, AT12 7PL	(01231) 485967
AKHTAR, M,	44 Kent Road, Hinton, Essex, AT12 3KU	(01231) 440958
BRIDGES, D,	25 Bond Street, Hinton, Essex, AT12 9OP	(01231) 439472
CHEUNG, C,	Flat 3, Fern Court, Pine Walk, Hinton, Essex, AT12 8LJ	(01231) 394810
COOK, C,	31 Queens Road, Hinton, Essex, AT12 4MJ	(01231) 728163
COOPER, A,	14 Tower Lane, Hinton, Essex, AT12 5HG	(01231) 473620
CROSS, S,	37 Queens Road, Hinton, Essex, AT12 4MJ	(01231) 384910
ELDERTON, M,	Everglades, 3 Riverside, Hinton, Essex, AT12 1PT	(01231) 759483
FERRARO, L,	12a Sunnyside Drive, Hinton, Essex, AT12 5DG	(01231) 747738
HOLMES, J,	1 Dukes Court, New Street, Hinton, Essex, AT12 7IJ	(01231) 488294
HUSSAIN, D,	99 Kingswood Crescent, Hinton, Essex, AT12 7DR	(01231) 401938
KAVANAGH, R,	15 Long Road, Hinton, Essex, AT12 1OL	(01231) 485994
KHALID, S,	42 Bond Street, Hinton, Essex, AT12 9KR	(01231) 374822
OAKLEY, S,	Flat 18, Fern Court, Pine Walk, Hinton, Essex, AT12 8LJ	(01231) 728362
PIGGOTT, C,	43 Ross Road, Hinton, Essex, AT12 9PD	(01231) 451436
POULTON, A,	34 Cox Court, New Street, Hinton, Essex, AT12 2IL	(01231) 374856
SMITH, M,	34b Park Road, Hinton, Essex, AT12 8AD	(01231) 737265
STEWART, L,	165 High Street, Hinton, Essex, AT12 2AH	(01231) 746302
WILLIAMS, S,	4 Queens Avenue, Hinton, Essex, AT12 4MX	(01231) 346832

Text © 2007, Sue Taylor

Annotations (right side):
- helps reader to trace across to number
- synonyms for 'Road'
- no 'Road' part; suggests street runs beside river
- town
- county
- postcode – first part refers to town; second part to road
- phone number – first part is area code; second part is individual house's number

Annotations (left side):
- 2nd-letter order needed
- bold capitals to stand out
- number of flat within large house or block of flats
- 4th-letter order needed
- house name
- might be flat or house divided into two, or new development on single site
- house number
- name of road
- surname given first, then initial of first name
- commas separate parts of address that would be on a new line on envelope

2: 2: **T18:** to use other alphabetically ordered texts

2: 2: **S7:** to investigate and recognise a range of other ways of presenting texts

Class 2 library catalogue
by Sue Taylor

Background
This text lists books in an imaginary class library, organised in alphabetical order by author surname. Public libraries and many school and class libraries are organised in this way so the text will give children a relevant context for alphabetical order. Many of the titles and authors will be familiar so the text will allow discussion about favourite stories and will help to promote positive attitudes to books and reading.

What's on the CD-ROM
This is also an extract from a library catalogue. It lists fewer books and is presented as book covers to stress the context. The books are organised in alphabetical order by author surname as in the core text, but there is only one name for any letter of the alphabet, so ordering is by initial letter only. The alphabet is on the page for reference. Children will be able to engage in discussion about books and authors. The text can be used in guided sessions focused on alphabetical order, and some of the same word-level objectives can be met.

Discussing the text
● Show and read the text and then focus on the title (explaining *catalogue*) and introductory sentences. Highlight the exclamation mark to emphasise the importance of the request. Ask the children what they think the purpose of this list is. Share children's experience of libraries, in and out of school.

● Read the list of authors and books. You might just show the authors or the books at first to encourage the children to share their knowledge and opinions.

● Demonstrate syllabic segmentation of some of the surnames – clap and count syllables, then recognise the syllable boundaries in the written word.

● Identify the alphabetical ordering by author surname (using second or third letter in some cases). Explain that books in libraries are often organised in this way. If relevant, this can be related to the previous text, the class directory, although noting that these well-known names are written in full as people will know them.

● Note the use of full capitals for the surnames, making them stand out on the page (as this is what people will use for searching). Also highlight the main words in titles with initial capitals but not the 'little' words.

● Identify the 'air' phoneme orally in *Pear* and *Bear* and then highlight the rime in each word. Also note *Dear* with the same rime but a different sound. Now pick out *-air* in *Hairy* and *Dairy* and, *-ere* in *Where*. Ask the children to think of other words with this sound and make lists according to spelling patterns.

Talk, read and write
● Ask the children to discuss in groups their favourite books and authors. They can share these with the rest of the class, using a 'talking frame' such as *'My favourite book (or author) is… because…'* Conduct a survey of favourite books and order them according to popularity.

● Ask the children to organise books in the class library in alphabetical order by author surname. This could be differentiated by giving groups particular sets of books. The books can then be listed in a catalogue for reference, perhaps in categories – funny/adventure/animal books, for example.

● In guided reading, discuss other information about a book that a reader might find useful in a library catalogue, such as the illustrator or how many pages. You might also discuss other features of book covers, such as a blurb, ISBN number and bar code.

● If possible, visit a local library or the main school library and talk to librarians about the organisation of books. If appropriate this could be extended to non-fiction books, introducing a simple Dewey system.

● In mixed-ability pairs, ask children to generate words with the 'air' phoneme, using different onsets and then categorise them by spelling pattern. They could make spelling posters, identifying words that are spelled with each rime.

Extension
Ask children to design a jacket for their favourite book, including all relevant features. These can be displayed in author alphabetical order.

Encourage children to make lists of books they have at home, or using home–school reading diaries to create their own catalogues.

2: 2: W2: to know the common spelling patterns for the vowel phonemes 'air'

2: 2: S7: to investigate and recognise a range of other ways of presenting texts

adds emphasis to sentence/ request

same spelling pattern but different sound

book titles in italic to make them distinctive

same 'air' sound but different spelling patterns

main words in titles have initial cap

Class 2 library catalogue

These books are in the blue box.
Please make sure you put them back in the right place so that other children can find the books they want.

Allan **AHLBERG**	*Each Peach, Pear, Plum*
Jez **ALBOROUGH**	*Duck in the Truck*
Anthony **BROWNE**	*Willy the Wimp*
John **BURNINGHAM**	*Mr Gumpy's Outing*
Rod **CAMPBELL**	*Dear Zoo*
Eric **CARLE**	*The Very Hungry Caterpillar*
Lynley **DODD**	*Hairy Maclary from Donaldson's Dairy*
Julia **DONALDSON**	*The Gruffalo*
Eric **HILL**	*Where's Spot?*
Pat **HUTCHINS**	*Rosie's Walk*
David **MCKEE**	*Elmer*
Jill **MURPHY**	*Peace at Last*
Michael **ROSEN**	*We're Going on a Bear Hunt*
Maurice **SENDAK**	*Where the Wild Things Are*
Martin **WADDELL**	*Farmer Duck*

Text © 2007, Sue Taylor

gives context and purpose for cataloguing

2nd-letter ordering

3rd-letter ordering

syllabic segmentation

familiar word

alphabetical order by author surname

surname in full caps to stand out; first name with initial cap

2: 2: T18: to use other alphabetically ordered texts

2: 2: W5: to discriminate, orally, syllables in multi-syllabic words

Catalogue index by Scholastic Ltd

Background

A shopping catalogue is likely to be a familiar context to many children. The main extract is from the *Toys* section of the index and is therefore likely to be of particular interest. Some of the brand names might be more familiar to children than to teachers. The index can be seen to contain much more detail than the contents list.

What's on the CD-ROM

A simplified version of the same text is provided to enable less able readers to engage with the same text type, but with fewer reading demands. The contents list is retained, but the index contains fewer items and lets children practise alphabetical order by first letter only. The text can be used in guided reading to investigate presentational features and word-level objectives for reading and spelling.

Discussing the text

● Show the text and read the main title. Ask the children what type of text this is and where it comes from. Share experiences of using shopping catalogues.

● Read the list of contents and check understanding of the broad categories. Ask the children to suggest items that might be in particular sections. Elicit that the page number is the first page of each section and that there are many pages for each section. Talk about the use of the contents as a way of finding pages to browse through when not looking for something very specific.

● Now look at the index extract. Use the contents to show that it is from the *Toys* section. Encourage brief talk about favourite toys and games, and prompt the children to use alphabetical order to see if any of of their favourites are listed here. If not, in which section would they appear?

● Highlight a set of entries beginning with one letter, for example *b*, and practise second- and third-letter ordering.

● Reinforce the different uses of a contents list and an index by pointing out that the contents are listed in *numerical* order, by page number, and the index is in *alphabetical* order.

● Read the full list and note that some entries are brand names. Briefly discuss the difference between general and specific, for example *Dolls/Accessories* and *Bratz*.

● Ask the children on which page you would find, for example, *Bob the Builder*. Repeat with other items, discussing specific features as they arise, such as multiple page ranges (separated by commas) and main page numbers given in bold type.

● Discuss the use of the oblique (/) in some entries (for example *Audio/CD/DVD*) as a shorthand way to denote *and/or*. Consider the reason for reversing the order of words in *Games, Boxed* and *Karaoke, Children's* (putting the main 'searchable' word first). If appropriate, relate this to the method of putting the surname first in directories (see page 54).

● Model the use of syllabic segmentation to read some of the longer words, clapping and counting syllables, then identifying the syllable boundaries in the written words, for example *El-ec-tron-ic*.

Talk, read and write

● Hand out cut up copies of the text for re-ordering alphabetically. This can be differentiated by varying the demand of first-, second- or third-letter ordering.

● Challenge small groups to find page numbers for specified entries as quickly as possible, and to go on to challenge each other in the same way. This could also be done with other shopping catalogues if available.

● Organise a class survey of favourite toys. The results could be presented in graphs or pictograms and arranged alphabetically. Alternatively, children could draw and label their favourite toy and these could be displayed alphabetically.

● In guided reading, practise counting syllables orally, and then matching this to the written words, using the children's names as a starting point.

Extension

Ask children to write (or draw) some of their toys and games at home or ones they might like to play with. Ask them to arrange them alphabetically, as in a catalogue (with made-up page numbers). Encourage children to bring in old catalogues from home for display and for practise in using the contents and indexes.

Text © 2007, Scholastic Ltd; photos in yellow panel: top left © Julie Elliot, top right © Marja Flick-Buijs, middle centre and middle right © Davide Guglielmo, middle left © Sarah Joos, top centre © Jeff Osborn, bottom centre © Jean Scheijen, middle left © Luis Rock, bottom right © Barb Ballard © Andrzej Pobiedzinski; photos in green panel: top left © Erke Taristse, middle right © Jeff Osborn, bottom left © Barbara Bar, bottom right

2: 2: W4: to split familiar oral and written compounds into their component parts

2: 2: S8: to use commas to separate items in a list

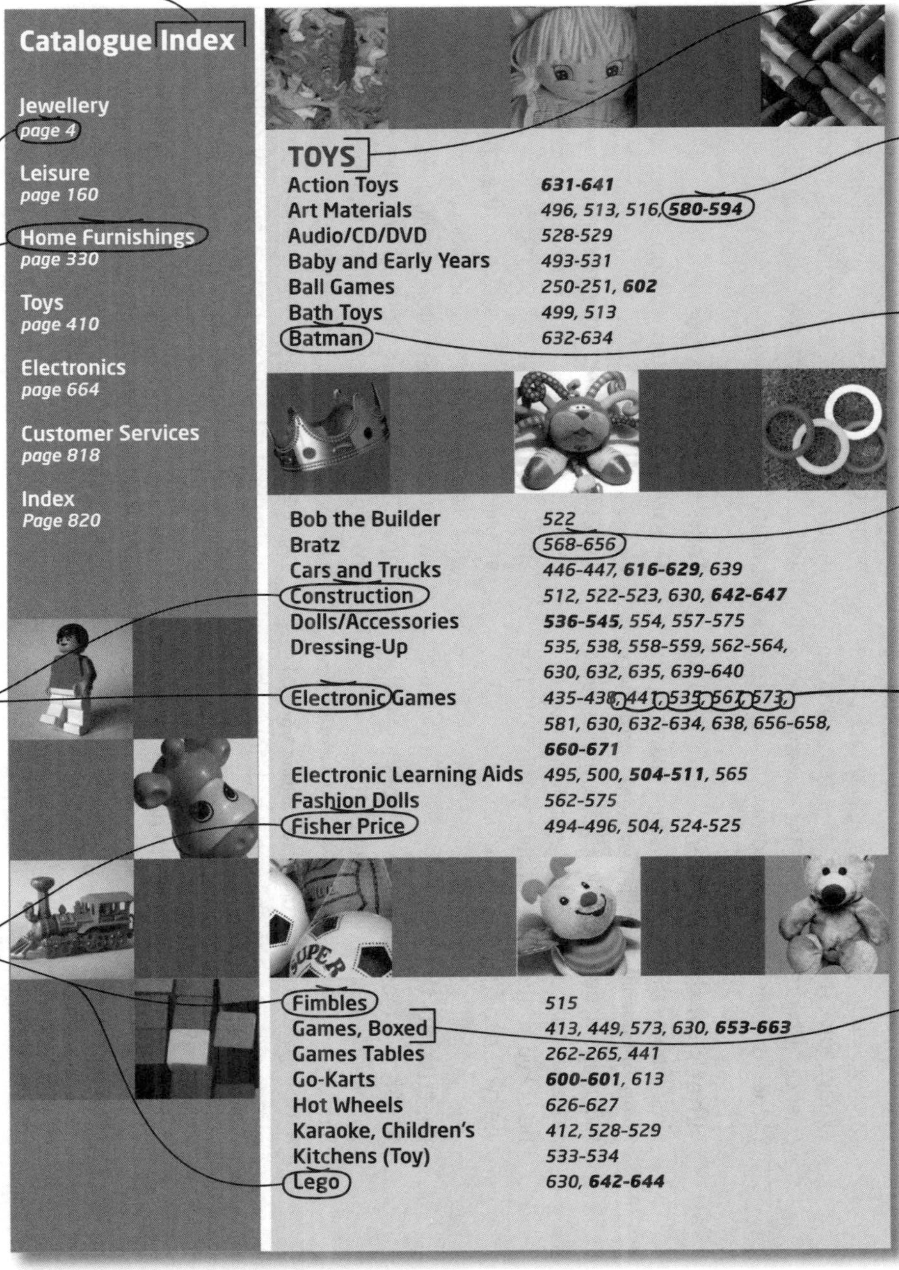

2: 2: T18: to use other alphabetically ordered texts

2: 2: W5 to discriminate, orally, syllables in multi-syllabic words

2: 2: S7: to investigate and recognise a range of other ways of presenting texts

title in big bold letters

bold number ranges indicate main pages for this category

compound word

several pages include these items; first and last pages shown here

commas separate pages, or ranges of pages, within a list

reader is more likely to look up 'Games' than 'Boxed Games'

detailed list of pages, always alphabetical, much more detailed than contents

first page of section given

broad categories allow reader to browse section

split into syllables for ease of reading

brand names

Catalogue Index

TOYS

Action Toys	**631-641**
Art Materials	496, 513, 516, **580-594**
Audio/CD/DVD	528-529
Baby and Early Years	493-531
Ball Games	250-251, **602**
Bath Toys	499, 513
Batman	632-634

Bob the Builder	522
Bratz	568-656
Cars and Trucks	446-447, **616-629**, 639
Construction	512, 522-523, 630, **642-647**
Dolls/Accessories	**536-545**, 554, 557-575
Dressing-Up	535, 538, 558-559, 562-564, 630, 632, 635, 639-640
Electronic Games	435-436, 441, 453, 561, 671, 581, 630, 632-634, 638, 656-658, **660-671**
Electronic Learning Aids	495, 500, **504-511**, 565
Fashion Dolls	562-575
Fisher Price	494-496, 504, 524-525

Fimbles	515
Games, Boxed	413, 449, 573, 630, **653-663**
Games Tables	262-265, 441
Go-Karts	**600-601**, 613
Hot Wheels	626-627
Karaoke, Children's	412, 528-529
Kitchens (Toy)	533-534
Lego	630, **642-644**

Glossary and index
by Sue Taylor

Background

Glossaries and indexes are alphabetically ordered texts often found in non-fiction books. A glossary gives a definition or information about vocabulary in a text, and an index allows a reader to find specific topics. Children need to be taught the use and purpose of glossaries and indexes to help them access texts about topics of interest. These extracts are from a book about frogs and can be linked to the next extract, on 'The life cycle of a frog', and to science. Children can use the glossary as a model for their own definitions.

What's on the CD-ROM

Simplified versions of the same extracts are given here. They have fewer items, to reduce the reading demands, and both are ordered alphabetically by first letter only. The text can be linked to the differentiated version of 'The life cycle of a frog' (see page 62).

Discussing the text

● Show the text and establish existing knowledge and experience of glossaries and an indexes. Note that glossaries give *definitions* and *explanations*, similar to subject-specific dictionaries. Ask the children which topic they think these extracts are from.

● If possible, show children a range of glossaries and indexes (and contents pages if appropriate) in non-fiction books, to establish where they are usually found.

● Read the glossary, demonstrating strategies for reading unfamiliar words, such as clapping and counting syllables, then identifying these in the written word.

● Share knowledge of the topic, and encourage children to add further explanations to some of the definitions. (Some of the words in this glossary appear in the following text.)

● Look at the order of entries in the glossary, exploring ordering by letters beyond the first, for example in *camouflage* and *carnivores*.

● Re-read the first entry. Ask the children if the definition is a full sentence. Show that, by itself, it does not make complete sense, although it has a capital letter and full stop, but it is enough for us to understand the headword. Model how to make a sentence by incorporating the headword *adult* (*An adult is…*). A different

model is needed for the verb *hatch* (*To hatch is to come out of an egg*).

● Now focus on the index, explaining any unfamiliar vocabulary. Note that some words in the index have explanations in the glossary.

● Look at the layout of the index, noting that words beginning with the same letter are grouped to help the reader to find a particular entry, and within the group, words are ordered alphabetically. Elicit what the numbers refer to, including the ranges, and test understanding by asking children to tell you which pages particular topics are on.

Talk, read and write

● Give the children cut up copies of the glossary and/or index to reassemble into alphabetical order, differentiated by the sections given. You could also ask children to match words to their definitions.

● Allocate words or topics to the children, after taking suggestions, in order to make an illustrated class glossary for use within a science topic. Provide dictionaries and other books on the topic to supplement the information given here and in the following text. Some children might be able to write definitions for terms in the index that do not have a glossary entry, such as *camouflage* or *predators*.

● Ask the children to turn glossary entries into complete sentences, using the model from shared reading. Ask response partners to check each other's sentences.

● Give the children cards with words from the glossary and a dictionary. They can compete in pairs to find entries and read out page numbers or definitions.

● Display a range of non-fiction books, on this topic or another relevant context, and ask them to record which books have an index and a glossary (and a contents page if appropriate). This record can be used as a reference for users of the books.

Extension

Ask children to list words related to area of interest and arrange them in alphabetical order. Some children could draw each item and some could write definitions. Group the lists into different topics and compile them into a reference book for the class book corner.

2: 2: T17: to know that glossaries give definitions and explanations

page numbers to show where that topic is mentioned

alphabetical order; grouped by first letter – makes it easier to find an entry

examples to help understand explanation

definition or explanation not full sentence

a kind of subject-specific dictionary

2: 2: T16: to use dictionaries and glossaries to locate words by using initial letter

2: 2: T18: to use other alphabetically ordered texts

ie, eats other animals; antonym is 'herbivore'

'let' – suffix meaning 'little'

compound word

birds and reptiles also lay eggs

ie, when it has just hatched

2: 2: W5: to discriminate, orally, syllables in multi-syllabic words

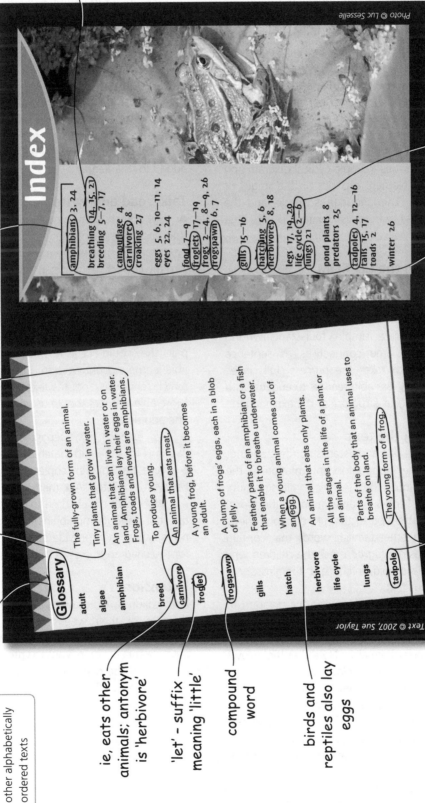

Index

amphibians 3, 24

breathing 14, 15, 21
breeding 5–7, 17

camouflage 4
carnivores 8
croaking 27

eggs 5, 6, 10–11, 14
eyes 22, 24

food 7–9
froglets 17–19
frogs 2–4, 8–9, 26
frogspawn 6, 7

gills 15–16

hatching 5, 6
herbivores 8, 18

legs 17, 19, 20
life cycle 2–6
lungs 21

pond plants 8
predators 25

tadpoles 4, 12–16
tails 15, 17
toads 2

winter 26

Photo © Luc Sesselle

pages 2, 3, 4, 5 and 6

words that are also in glossary

Glossary

adult   The fully-grown form of an animal.

algae   Tiny plants that grow in water.

amphibian   An animal that can live in water or on land. Amphibians lay their eggs in water. Frogs, toads and newts are amphibians.

breed   To produce young.

carnivore   An animal that eats meat.

froglet   A young frog, before it becomes an adult.

frogspawn   A clump of frogs' eggs, each in a blob of jelly.

gills   Feathery parts of an amphibian or a fish that enable it to breathe underwater.

hatch   When a young animal comes out of an egg.

herbivore   An animal that eats only plants.

life cycle   All the stages in the life of a plant or an animal.

lungs   Parts of the body that an animal uses to breathe on land.

tadpole   The young form of a frog.

Text © 2007, Sue Taylor

2: 2: T20: to make class dictionaries or glossaries of special interest words, giving explanations and definitions

2: 2: S9: to secure the use of simple sentences in own writing

The life cycle of a frog
by Sue Taylor

Background

This explanatory text links to the glossary and index from a non-fiction book about frogs (see page 60). Definitions of some of the vocabulary in this text (in bold) can be found in that glossary. The text might also be linked to the following one on the life cycle of a chicken (page 64). It is of particular relevance in the spring term and, if your school has a pond, the process can be observed in the natural habitat. (It is possible to hatch and keep tadpoles in an aquarium until they have both pairs of legs.) The text provides a simple cyclical diagram and the written element expands on the stages of the process. The language is simple, and the chronological nature is reinforced by time connectives.

What's on the CD-ROM

This text includes the same cyclical diagram as the core text to enable children to explore the process by interpreting the diagram. The text then provides a simple four-stage writing frame, using time connectives as sentence starters, which takes the process 'full circle'. This will allow less able readers to engage with the chronological structure of the explanation.

Discussing the text

● Read the title and establish understanding.
● Read the introductory information in the box. Highlight the technical classification, *amphibian*. Model syllabification of the word, and draw attention to the 'ph' digraph, briefly considering other familiar words that contain this, such as *photograph*. Ask the children why this word is in bold, referring to the glossary in the previous text.
● Then ask pairs to describe the diagram to each other. Ask the children how they 'read' the diagram. Where did they start? Why? Could you start anywhere else? Note that the arrows take the reader in a *clockwise* circle (hence *cycle*), with no beginning or end, although it seems most logical to start with the frog.
● Now read the text, drawing out that this *explains*, and expands, the diagram. Check the vocabulary in bold in the glossary (previous text), and discuss any other unfamiliar terms.
● Relate the written text to the stages in the diagram, drawing attention to information in the text that is not in the illustration. You may find it helpful to draw (or ask children to) the 'interim' stages to reinforce understanding.
● Highlight some of the time connectives. Ask the children what they have in common, then find other examples and discuss how they reinforce the order in which things happen. Identify the time scale of events, noting how long each stage lasts (for example, eggs hatch after ten days, tadpoles stay in the water for ten weeks, frogs first lay eggs when they are two or three years old). 'Time' labels could be added to the diagram.

Talk, read and write

● Ask the children to cut up their pictures so that each one is on a separate piece of paper. Ask them to shuffle them then re-order them into the correct sequence, in a circle. Add paper arrows to identify the cycle.
● Model writing a sentence to act as a caption to one picture and ask the children to caption each picture. If the children work in pairs they could act as response partners. Less able learners could work in a guided group or match sentences from the text to their pictures. More able learners should use time connectives and add detail.
● To extend this, separate pictures and captions for others to match and sequence.
● Give the children copies of the text with key words omitted. Ask them to fill the gaps.
● Work with the children to generate a list of questions about amphibians that this text does not answer. Then provide a range of resources for the children to research their questions.

Extension

Ask children to draw and label a cyclical diagram of their week at home and/or at school, with one picture for each of the seven days. Some children could write captions to accompany the diagram, such as *On Sunday I play football*.

2: 2: W3: to read and spell words containing the digraph 'ph'

2: 2: T19: to read flow charts and cyclical diagrams that explain a process

2: 2: S9: to secure the use of simple sentences in own writing

2: 2: T21: to produce simple flow charts or diagrams that explain a process

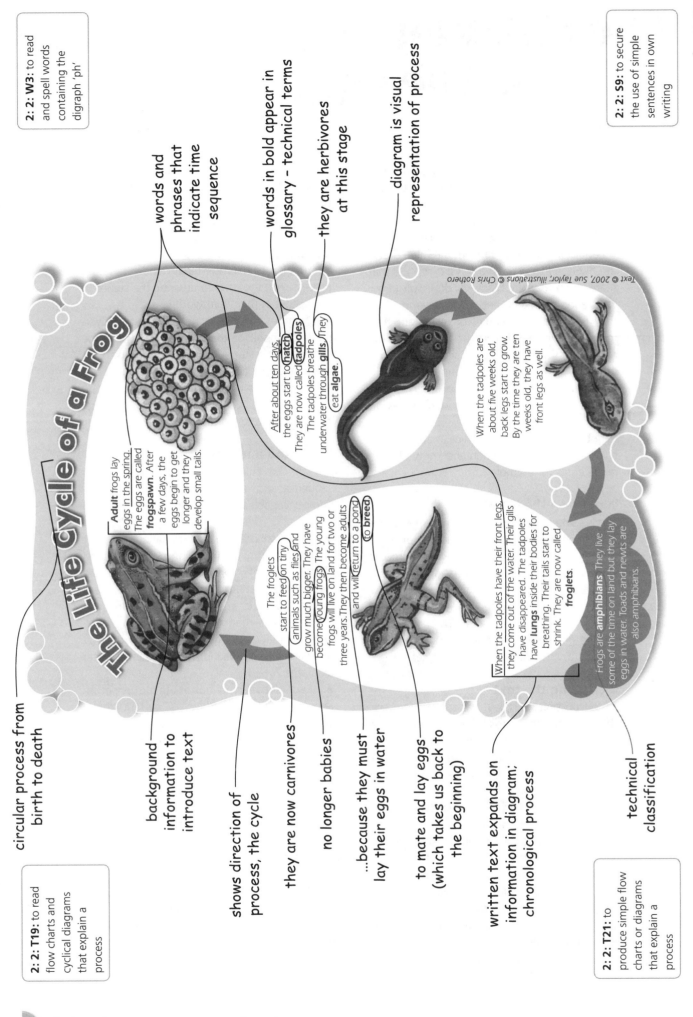

The Life Cycle of a Frog

Adult frogs lay eggs in the spring. The eggs are called **frogspawn**. After a few days, the eggs begin to get longer and they develop small tails.

After about ten days, the eggs start to **hatch**. They are now called **tadpoles**. The tadpoles breathe underwater through **gills**. They eat **algae**.

When the tadpoles are about five weeks old, back legs start to grow. By the time they are ten weeks old, they have front legs as well.

When the tadpoles have their front legs, they come out of the water. Their gills have disappeared. The tadpoles have **lungs** inside their bodies for breathing. Their tails start to shrink. They are now called **froglets**.

The froglets start to feed on tiny animals such as flies and grow much bigger. The young become young frogs. The young frogs will live on land for two or three years. They then become adults and will return to a pond to breed.

Frogs are **amphibians**. They live some of the time on land but they lay eggs in water. Toads and newts are also amphibians.

Text © 2007, Sue Taylor, illustrations © Chris Rothero

circular process from birth to death

words and phrases that indicate time sequence

words in bold appear in glossary – technical terms

they are herbivores at this stage

diagram is visual representation of process

background information to introduce text

shows direction of process, the cycle

they are now carnivores

no longer babies

...because they must lay their eggs in water

to mate and lay eggs (which takes us back to the beginning)

written text expands on information in diagram; chronological process

technical classification

The chicken or the egg? by Sue Taylor

Background

This explanatory text describes the life cycle of a chicken (which applies to most birds), and can be linked to the previous extract on the life cycle of a frog. The text uses captioned photographs to describe the process in a series of logical steps, introducing subject-specific vocabulary. The quandary in the title draws attention to the fact that this is a cycle, and that there is no answer. Many children will know little about chickens and eggs beyond what they find in a supermarket or restaurant. The text will therefore develop knowledge of the natural world and link to a science topic on growth. Children will need to understand that the eggs they eat could not grow into chickens. The text could also tie in with issues in citizenship on animal welfare: some children might be aware of the ethical debates over chicken and egg production and know of free-range eggs, for example.

What's on the CD-ROM

This is a simpler version of the same explanation. The same photographs are used but with shorter captions that describe the process without supplementary information. Less able readers will be able to engage with the key objectives and be involved in discussion topics without the reading demands. The text can be used in guided reading and writing to explore explanatory texts and cyclical processes.

Discussing the text

● If possible, display various images of chickens and other birds. Show the title of the text and explain the nature of this age-old quandary. Elicit children's understanding of where chickens and eggs come. You might at this stage draw a very simple cyclical diagram of *chicken > egg > chicken* and tell children that the text explains this process.

● Read the introduction and encourage the children to share their knowledge of birds and nests. Children may need assistance to connect chickens with other birds. You might introduce the word *hen* as an alternative, to distinguish (but also make the connection) between the live bird and the meat we eat. If appropriate, you might discuss the way chickens and eggs are mass-produced.

● Discuss each picture and its caption in turn. Discuss meanings of technical vocabulary and new concepts.

● Ask pairs of children to identify two or three key words in each caption that explain the process. Make a class list to include, for example, *chicken, lays eggs, nest, hatch*. Note that most of the captions include additional information to help the reader understand the process. Ask the pairs to describe the stages to each other in their own words.

● Number the pictures and captions as you read, to emphasise the sequential stages in the process – one stage leading on to the next. At the final stage, add an arrow to show that this stage leads back to the first one again. Rearrange the pictures and text in a circle, adding arrows to indicate the cycle.

Talk, read and write

● Let the children work independently to sequence and match captions to pictures, or add key vocabulary to a version of the text with gaps.

● Some children could draw and label their own diagrams of the process, including illustrations of supplementary information given in the text. Prompt them to use the class list of words in their captions. Remind the children to re-read their sentences for sense and punctuation. Some children could research other life cycles, drawing and labeling cyclical diagrams.

● In guided reading look at other explanatory texts, perhaps related to a current topic. Encourage children to ask 'how' and 'why' questions, such as *Why do the seasons change?* or *How did the Fire of London start?* As appropriate, children could then research answers.

● In shared and guided writing, revisit technical vocabulary highlighted earlier and write definitions for a class dictionary or glossary, to be organised in alphabetical order.

Extension

Ask children to list words related to something they enjoy doing and to write a definition of each. Some children might just draw labelled pictures. These could be put into alphabetical order to make a glossary.

2: 2: T20: to make class dictionaries and glossaries of special interest words, giving explanations and definitions

2: 2: S9: to secure the use of simple sentences in own writing

common 'philosophical' question; title in form of question engages reader

chickens don't fly well

might be more or fewer

scientific vocabulary – developing egg

scientific vocabulary – to break out of shell

...from the inside

shell is hard for protection from outside; chick is tiny and still weak

chicken is now grown up, an adult

cycle begins again

Text © 2007, Sue Taylor; photos: eggs © Miguel Ugalde, chickens on nest and chick with egg © Joszef Szasz-Fabian, baby chick and chicken © Kate Childers

Which comes first – the chicken or the egg?

A chicken is a bird. All birds lay eggs, usually in nests. Nests may be in trees or on the ground.

The female chicken makes a nest on the ground and lays her eggs in it. She usually lays about ten eggs.

She sits on the eggs to keep them warm and protect them. Inside each egg the baby chicken begins to grow. It is called an embryo.

When the chick is ready to hatch it uses a special tooth to break a hole in the shell. When the hole is big enough, the chick struggles out.

Baby chicks don't have proper feathers. They have a soft, fluffy coat called down. Feathers grow when the young chicken is a few weeks old.

When the chicken is about five months old she is ready to lay eggs.

short introduction on chickens and eggs

the 'lady' chicken, the 'mum'

diagrams help reader to interpret text

'keep them safe'

usual name for a baby chicken

this falls off later – chickens don't have teeth

scientific vocabulary – first 'coat' (of chicken)

written text works as captions to pictures

2: 2: T19: to read flow charts and cyclical diagrams that explain a process

2: 2: T21: to produce simple flow charts or diagrams that explain a process

How does your garden grow?

by Sue Taylor

Background

This text explains the life cycle of a flowering plant and links to science topics on plants and growth, particularly relevant in the spring term. This particular context might also be linked to healthy eating. A bean can be grown successfully in the classroom in the early stages, and if it is planted outside to reach maturity, children can be involved in the complete cycle. The stages of the process are explained here in simple language, while introducing subject-specific vocabulary, and pictures support the written text. The introduction gives background information about beans and how to grow them. Children will be able to identify the key stages in the process and represent them as a cyclical diagram.

What's on the CD-ROM

This is a simpler version, supported by the same illustrations. The steps in the process are described clearly without supplementary information but retain key vocabulary, and are identified by time connectives to reinforce the sequence. Less able readers can benefit from the additional information in the core text through shared reading, and in guided sessions will be able to use the differentiated text to produce cyclical diagrams.

Discussing the text

● If possible, have examples of different types of beans and peas and other seeds on display. Show and discuss the text title, noting that the question involves the reader.

● Share experiences of plant growth and of beans (including baked beans). Explain that beans grow in pods on flowering plants and that this text explains how this happens. Connect to other explanatory texts read, noting that they answer 'how' or 'why' questions.

● Read the introductory paragraphs, noting how this information and advice makes the reader want to be involved in the process. Clarify any vocabulary or concepts, using dictionaries or glossaries, as needed, to find explanations of technical terms.

● Cover the written text initially and reveal the pictures one at a time. Ask the children to to *describe* what each picture shows, prompting the use of appropriate vocabulary. Then reveal

the text. Compare this with children's descriptions, noting particularly the language of the text, which *explains* what happens. Explain the functions of parts of a plant at an appropriate level.

● Go through the natural sequence of stages in the process, showing how each stage leads to the next. For example, the roots grow first to draw up water; then the shoot grows towards the light, which is needed so the leaves can produce food for the plant.

● Highlight the connectives that indicate the chronological sequence of the steps. Consider the way in which the final sentence takes us back to the first step and, therefore, the cycle begins again. Add arrows to represent this.

● At word level, highlight the different letter combinations that represent the 'ee' phoneme in *bean* and *seed*. Ask the children to find other words in the text with either of these spelling patterns. Compile two lists.

Talk, read and write

● Hand out enlarged copies of the pictures from the text and paper arrows. Ask the children to put the pictures in sequence and then arrange them in a circle with arrows to represent the cycle. Then ask them to label the pictures with key words.

● Model writing captions to explain the stages in the process, which the children can continue independently. More able learners could include additional information to make their explanations more interesting.

● Ask the children to write simple definitions for key vocabulary from the text. Some children can use reference sources to write their own definitions. Less able readers could be given words and/or pictures to match to definitions. From this, compile a class glossary.

● Ask the children to generate a list of words containing the 'ee' phoneme and to arrange them in the two spelling patterns. Alternatively, give key words from which to generate rhyming families, such as *seed* and *meet*.

Extension

Ask children to practise spelling key topic words. To put the words in context, encourage the children to find pictures of flowering plants in magazines or catalogues to label for display.

2: 2: T20: to make class dictionaries and glossaries of special interest words, giving explanations and definitions

more specific – works as subheading

text and images work together to describe process

connectives indicating chronological sequence

beginning of stem; very first green growth

seed containers

linking back to beginning of process – shows cyclical nature

2: 2: W10: to learn new words from reading linked to particular topics

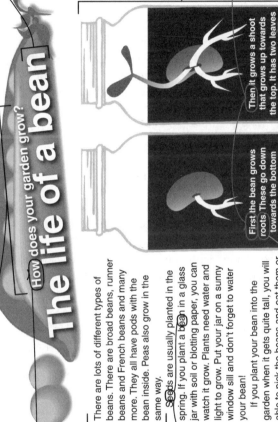

2: 2: T19: to read flow charts and cyclical diagrams that explain a process

title in form of question engages reader

indicates this will be an explanatory text

2: 2: T21: to produce simple flow charts or diagrams that explain a process

general information and advice about growing beans

different spellings of 'ee' long vowel phoneme

these draw up water and minerals (food)

main stem

...because it needs more room and more food from the soil

2: 2: W1: to secure reading and spelling of words containing different spellings of the long vowel phonemes from Year 1

How does your garden grow?
The life of a bean

There are lots of different types of beans. There are broad beans, runner beans and French beans and many more. They all have pods with the bean inside. Peas also grow in the same way.

Seeds are usually planted in the spring. If you plant a bean in a glass jar with soil or blotting paper, you can watch it grow. Plants need water and light to grow. Put your jar on a sunny window sill and don't forget to water your bean!

If you plant your bean into the garden when it gets quite tall, you will able to pick the beans and eat them or grow some more plants!

First the bean grows roots. These go down towards the bottom of the jar.

Then it grows a shoot that grows up towards the top. It has two leaves at the end of the shoot.

More leaves grow as the plant gets taller. You should plant it in the garden now.

Now flowers grow on the stalk. Each flower makes a bean.

When the flowers die, the pods start to grow. The pods grow bigger and inside there are new bean seeds. You can eat these or save some and plant them next year to grow new plants.

Where does bread come from?

by Sue Taylor

Background

Most children will have eaten bread in various forms. Some will even have made it (see the text for making bread on page 18). Children might know that bread is made from flour (as are biscuits and cakes, for example), but might not know where flour comes from. The text will develop general knowledge and can be linked to science work on plants and growth, and to the previous text on the life cycle of a bean. This simple explanatory text describes the process from wheat to bread with subject-specific vocabulary. The introduction gives additional background information to 'set the scene'. The four key stages in the process are illustrated to support the written explanation.

What's on the CD-ROM

This is a simplified version of the core text, to enable less able readers to meet similar objectives. The introduction is greatly reduced and acts as a caption for the illustrations. The stages are described in short, simple sentences, which nevertheless retain key vocabulary. The process is sub-divided into two parts for added clarity. This text can be used in guided reading and writing to explore the process and features of explanatory texts.

Discussing the text

● Read the title, without revealing the rest of the text, and establish existing knowledge by asking the children if they can answer the question.

● Read the introduction and model strategies for reading unfamiliar words. For example, demonstrate syllabic segmentation of words, orally initially, clapping and counting syllables, and then noting syllable boundaries.

● Highlight the function of the commas in the list of cereals and note the use of *and* instead of a comma before the last item.

● Encourage the children to talk about their favourite types of bread and how they eat it and make links to healthy eating. Explain the link between *cereal*, used here to describe particular types of plant, and breakfast foods.

● Discuss the images, asking children to describe to a partner in their own words what it shows and note that it explains a process visually.

● Now read the text, one stage at a time, discussing difficult concepts and using additional diagrams, if possible. You might demonstrate the process of grinding with a pestle and mortar.

● Number the stages or draw arrows between them to emphasise the order of events, noting that they follow each other in a natural and logical sequence, which is further reinforced through references to the seasons.

● Draw attention to *Where* in the title, and write suggestions for other question words on the board. Note that many of these words begin with *wh* (pronounced *w*, with a silent *h*), but noting exceptions *who* and *how*. Also ask the children to find other *wh* words in the text (*wheat* and *whole*), and note their different pronunciations.

Talk, read and write

● Use enlarged pictures of the four stages and use shared writing to compose one or two sentences to caption each picture. Encourage more able learners to add more detail.

● In guided writing, highlight key vocabulary and compose definitions for one or two, using dictionaries or other reference books if appropriate. Then ask the children to continue independently to create glossaries. Less able readers could match terms to prepared definitions or labels to pictures.

● Hand out key words from the text on large cards and, hiding the text, ask small groups to put the words in the order in which they occur in the process.

● Ask groups to discuss and list their favourite types of bread or breakfast cereal. Then ask them to turn their lists into sentences, using commas to separate the items.

● Ask the children to practise reading and spelling of appropriate words containing the 'wh' digraph. They could make wordsearches (using a modelled example), containing words they have learned, to challenge others.

Extension

Ask children to write sentences listing their favourite foods, clothes and so on. Some children might need a writing frame. Children could also write questions to ask family and friends, using question words.

2: 2: T20: to make class dictionaries and glossaries of special interest words, giving explanations and definitions

2: 2: W3: to read and spell words containing the diagraph 'wh'

2: 2: S8: to use commas to separate items in a list

bold indicates topic-specific terms

commas separate items in list: all types of cereal

particular type of seed

'meal' – another word for 'grain', so 'whole grain'

'wh' pronounced 'w' or 'h'

use syllabic segmentation

does lots of different jobs

not used for flour; often used for animal bedding

crushed

seasons show chronological order

Where does bread come from?

Bread is made from flour. Flour is made by grinding the **grain** (seeds) of plants called **cereals**. It is usually made from grains of wheat but it can also be made of oats, barley, rye or rice.

If the **wholegrain** is used, the flour is brown and it makes **wholemeal** bread. If only the inside of the grain is used the flour is white.

In the past, people used to grow their own wheat, and ground flour to make bread by hand. Nowadays farmers grow wheat in huge fields, and mills use **electric** mixing machines and **enormous** ovens to make hundreds of loaves of bread. You can buy **bakeries** or make your own flower and make your own bread.

In the **spring**, the farmer **sows** the seeds.

During the **summer** the seeds grow into tall plants. New seeds (grains) grow at the top of each plant stalk. In the **autumn** the farmer uses a **combine harvester** to cut the crop.

The **combine harvester** separates the grain from the **stalks**. The stalks are left in the fields. This is called **straw**.

The grain goes to a flour **mill**. Here it is **ground** into a fine powder called flour.

The flour is put into bags and sent to the **bakery** to be made into bread (and cakes, buns and biscuits).

Text © 2007, Sue Taylor; photos: wheat seeds © Elke Rohn, wheat © Simon Templar, flour © Melanie Martinelli, bread and rolls © 2006, Jupiter Images Corporation

text will answer this question

background information, including historical, about bread and flour; shows how things have changed

addressing reader directly and encouraging personal involvement

diagrams show four-step process

plants seeds

text also shows steps

make link to knowledge of harvest (festival)

2: 2: T19: to read flow charts and cyclical diagrams that explain a process

2: 2: T21: to produce simple flow charts or diagrams that explain a process

2: 2: W5: to discriminate, orally, syllables in multi-syllabic words

The journey of a letter
by Sue Taylor

Background

This text explains how a letter gets from the writer to its recipient, which in some cases is a remarkable journey! Most children will have written and posted cards or letters to friends and family, giving this text a meaningful context. It would be most effective if used in conjunction with a visit to a post office or linked to a topic on people in the local community. The text is organised in clear steps, using subheadings to identify them, and the explanations use simple language while introducing key vocabulary. Illustrations show the first and last stages of the journey. The text offers opportunities for children to learn to read and write their own addresses for a real purpose and might be used in conjunction with the directory extract on page 54.

What's on the CD-ROM

The same process is presented visually here, with a picture for each stage, under the same subheadings as the core text. Less able readers can therefore explore the process and engage with the explanation with less challenging text. The text can be used in guided sessions for sequencing and writing simple captions for each illustration.

Discussing the text

● If possible, display a range of letters and cards with envelopes. Read the title of the text and ask the children what they understand by it. Then read the first sentence, which asks a question. Note that this addresses the reader directly and indicates what the text will explain. Share children's answers to the 'how' question and make notes on the board.

● Read the next two sentences, which give background information that 'sets the scene'. Ask the children why this journey is described as a story, noting that this makes it sound exciting and like an adventure.

● Look at the top picture, identifying each part of the address and comparing it to children's own addresses. Recall the importance of the postcode for sorting mail. Discuss the purpose of the stamp, sharing understanding of first and second class if appropriate, and noting that this is how we pay for the postal service.

● Read and list the subheadings. Ask the children what they understand by each word, and challenge them to use each one in a phrase or sentence. Note that the subheadings summarise the stages of the journey, in order.

● Now read each stage of the journey, clarifying ideas and vocabulary to ensure understanding. Ask the children to explain each stage to a partner as you read. Draw a picture of each stage and place these under their subheadings (or use the differentiated text). See how well the children's predictions match up with the text.

● Finally, look at the bottom picture from the differentiated text. Compare the house number with that on the original letter to see how this completes the journey – the letter has reached its destination. Add arrows to the sequence to reinforce the order of events and that one event is dependent on the previous one.

Talk, read and write

● Let the children practise writing their own and their families' names and addresses. Give this a context by asking them to address an envelope, for a newsletter to be sent home for example. If possible, take children to the nearest postbox to post the letters and ask them to tell you when the letters arrive home.

● Give the children pictures of the journey to sequence and match to the subheadings picked out earlier, adding arrows between the pictures. Model writing one or two sentences as a caption for each picture. Children can then continue this independently, with the more able adding interesting details.

● In guided writing, highlight key vocabulary and write definitions for a class glossary on this topic.

Extension

Ask children to bring in a range of letters, cards and envelopes from home, with permission. Use these to discuss the different types and purposes of letters, and for display. If possible, label the envelopes or cards to identify different parts of the address. Children could also gather a list of places that family and friends send letters and cards to and plot these on maps to show the journeys made. Whose letter has made the longest journey?

2: 2: T20: to make class dictionaries and glossaries of special interest words, giving explanations and definitions

name, house number and road, town, county, postcode

question word; text will explain

sets the scene

to show you have paid for the service

collective term for all letters, cards and parcels (relate to email)

known as 'airmail'; most letters going abroad go by plane

subheadings summarise the stages of the journey

2: 2: W9: to spell common irregular words from Appendix List 1

The journey of a letter

Have you ever wondered how a letter or card gets to the person you have sent it to?

This is the story of the journey of a letter. Some letters travel just a short distance but others travel right across the world.

Posting

When you send a letter or card to someone, you write their name and address on the envelope. Then you stick a stamp on the envelope and put it in the post box.

Collecting

A postman collects all the letters from the post box and takes them to the nearest sorting office.

Sorting

At the sorting office the letters are put into different boxes according to where they are being sent.

Transporting

The mail is sent to the post office nearest to the address on the envelope. It might travel by van or train. If it is going abroad it may go by ship or by plane.

Sorting again

The letters are sorted again into bags for each postman or woman to deliver.

Delivery

The postman or woman puts the letter or card through the letter box of the right house.

Mina Akhtar,
44 Kent Road,
Hinton,
Essex, ATI2 3KR

Text © 2007, Sue Taylor; photo © 2006, Jupiter Images Corporation; illustration © Corel

letter travels from one place to another

question encourages response from reader

a real story; makes the journey sound like an exciting adventure

addressing reader makes it personal

main post office

usually by machine these days; machines read postcodes

postmen and women carry bags for their 'round'; they might go on foot, by bicycle or in a van

2: 2: T19: to read flow charts that explain a process

2: 2: T21: to produce simple flow charts or diagrams that explain a process

Touch

by Judy Tatchell and Alastair Smith

Background

This extract explains in simple terms how we register touch. It gives background information about the sense of touch and then uses a labelled illustration with an explanatory caption to describe how we feel pain. The cartoon-style illustrations are appealing and the language of the text is simple. Key technical terminology is used where relevant. The text will help children to use simple diagrams to explain processes, and it links to the investigation of senses in science. It also offers the opportunity to explore antonyms.

What's on the CD-ROM

This text uses only the labelled illustration and simple description of the process. Children can benefit from the additional information provided in the core text through shared reading (and in science lessons) and use the simplified text in guided reading to explain the process and in guided writing as a model for their own writing.

Discussing the text

● Read the title and ask the children what they already know about touch. (It is best if this text is read in conjunction with practical science investigations.) Say that the text will explain how the sense of touch works.

● Read the complete text, pointing to each part as you read. Then ask the children to tell their partners, in their own words, what it was about. Take feedback to establish children's comprehension.

● Now read the first part of the text again. Note that the pictures reinforce the vocabulary. Discuss the purpose of the ellipses here (to indicate a continuing list) and ask the children to suggest other *hot/cold*, *soft/hard*, *tickly/scratchy* things. Note that all parts of the body can feel but that hands (and particularly fingers) are most *sensitive*.

● The next section, identified by the subheading *Feeling things*, is the main explanation. Remind the children that explanatory texts describe how things work. Discuss the effect of the funny pictures in engaging the reader, and ask for suggestions of other painful things.

● Read and discuss the last section and ask

children to draw lines to match the text to elements of the diagram. Point out the arrows that indicate how the message is passed to the brain, and get them to trace the path on themselves or a partner, noting that the message would travel in a similar way from any part of the body. Ensure that the children appreciate that this is a simplified diagram.

● Focus again on *hot/cold* and *soft/hard*. Ask the children what is special about these pairs of words, recalling or introducing the word *antonym*. Ask them to think of other opposites that describe how things feel, for example *rough/smooth*, *wet/dry*. Extend this to the other senses, for example *loud/soft*, *light/dark*, *sweet/sour*. Gather a bank of topic words for reference.

Talk, read and write

● In shared writing, choose another context, such as stepping on a sharp stone, and model how to write an explanation of how the message gets from the foot to the brain. Add a labelled picture as in the core text to support the writing. Then encourage the children to choose their own context and write explanations, with labelled diagrams. Some children might prefer to just draw and label a diagram.

● Write definitions for the technical terms in the text to compile into a glossary. Some children might do this independently; others can be supported in guided writing.

● Help pairs of children to role play the sense of touch. One child should mime touching or being touched by something for their partner to guess what it is. Encourage them to extend this to other senses.

● Starting with 'senses words', ask the children to generate pairs of antonyms. Allow them to use dictionaries and thesauruses, if appropriate. Some children could be given words to find antonyms; some could be given antonym pairs to illustrate. Encourage more able learners to use the pairs in sentences, orally or in writing, to illustrate their meanings.

Extension

Ask children to bring in small items for a 'touch' display. Look particularly for opposites. Help the children to write captions for their items.

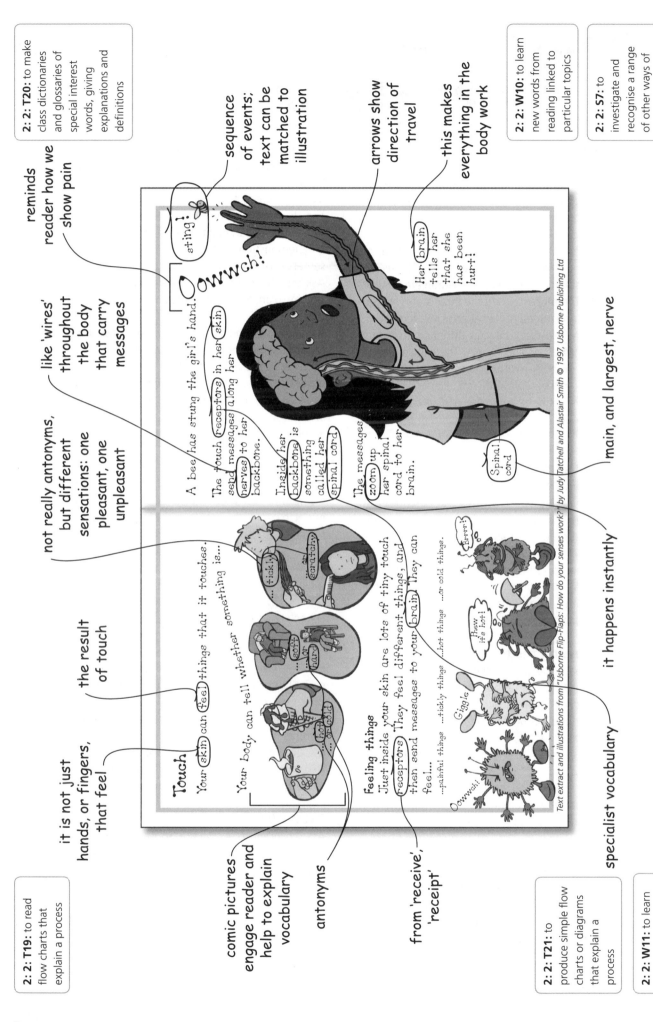

2: 2: T20: to make class dictionaries and glossaries of special interest words, giving explanations and definitions

reminds reader how we show pain

sequence of events; text can be matched to illustration

arrows show direction of travel

this makes everything in the body work

2: 2: W10: to learn new words from reading linked to particular topics

2: 2: S7: to investigate and recognise a range of other ways of presenting texts

like 'wires' throughout the body that carry messages

not really antonyms, but different sensations: one pleasant, one unpleasant

it is not just hands, or fingers, that feel

the result of touch

main, and largest, nerve

comic pictures engage reader and help to explain vocabulary

antonyms

from 'receive', 'receipt'

it happens instantly

specialist vocabulary

2: 2: T19: to read flow charts that explain a process

2: 2: T21: to produce simple flow charts or diagrams that explain a process

2: 2: W11: to learn the use of antonyms

Text extract and illustrations from "Usborne Flip-Flaps: How do your senses work?" by Judy Tatchell and Alastair Smith © 1997, Usborne Publishing Ltd

Change — ice, water, steam

by Sue Taylor

Background

This text explains a familiar natural process, linking to changing materials in science. Although some of the scientific concepts and vocabulary might be a little advanced for Year 2, the simplicity of the approach will make the text accessible to most children. Explanations of terms such as *solid*, *liquid* and *gas* will need to be related to materials that children are familiar with. The processes and the three states should be demonstrated, if not already investigated in a science lesson (drawing attention to safety issues when boiling water). The explanation is given in both written form and through a diagrammatic representation, allowing children to develop both language and visual literacy skills. Key concepts can be explored as pairs of opposites to further enhance understanding.

What's on the CD-ROM

The same topic is presented in simplified form on the CD-ROM. The written text describes just the key changes and is related very closely to the labelled diagram. Some of the more abstract scientific terminology has been omitted to reduce the reading demands. The text can be used in guided reading to explore the nature of explanatory texts and to develop visual literacy skills.

Discussing the text

● Read the title, *Change*, and encourage children to talk about their experiences of significant change. Relate to other topics studied if appropriate, such as weather.

● Introduce the subheading, *Ice, water, steam*, and establish children's knowledge of the relationship between these states and the significance of change in this context.

● Read the whole text, without showing the diagram at this stage, discussing concepts at an appropriate level. List key words on the board.

● Identify and discuss the structure of the text. Note that the first sentence is a general statement that introduces the topic – an *explanation* of the changes that occur when water is heated or cooled. The next two sentences describe the processes, the cause and effect. The fourth sentence introduces the second part of the explanation – the opposite cause and effect.

● Now explore the diagram, noting how the labelled arrows show the direction of change from water (the natural state). The labels on the diagram match the key words from the text. The diagram and the written text present the same information in different ways.

● Demonstrate how to match the first sentence of the explanation, to the diagram. Ask the children to work in pairs to match the other explanatory sentences to the appropriate parts.

● Highlight *colder* and *hotter* and ask the children what they notice, drawing out that they are opposites. Ask the children to find other opposites in the text (*Freezes/Boils*, *cools down/warms up*) and note that the text is about 'opposite' changes. Revise the word *antonym* and talk about other opposites.

Talk, read and write

● Give the children blank copies of the diagram to match or add labels. Some children might be able to write explanatory sentences for each. Encourage others to draw and label their own flow charts to describe the process.

● Discuss other changes, depending on topics studied, such as human growth, other plant or animal life cycles, the seasons, melting chocolate or ice cream. Model the construction of flow charts or diagrams, by drawing a series of pictures connected by arrows.

● Begin an illustrated class dictionary of key scientific vocabulary. Some children might write their own definitions after teacher modelling; others could match definitions or words to pictures.

● Create an antonym display or a thesaurus. Ask the children to find pairs of opposites and to illustrate them or use them in sentences.

Extension

Ask children to explain a routine at home. Suggest that they draw labelled pictures, using arrows to indicate the sequence. Some children could write sentences to accompany it.

2: 2: T20: to make class dictionaries and glossaries of special interest words, giving explanations and definitions

2: 2: W11: to learn the use of antonyms

what this text is about

general statement as introduction

visual representation of process

the three states that materials can be in; relate to water, ice, steam

CHANGE

Ice, water, steam

Water is a liquid that can change when it gets colder or hotter.

When water freezes, it changes into ice. Ice is a solid.

When water boils, it changes into steam. Steam is a gas.

These changes are reversible

Steam (gas) can change back into water (liquid) when it cools down.

Ice (solid) can change back into water (liquid) when it warms up.

WARMS

BOILS

water (liquid)

steam (gas)

ice (solid)

water (liquid)

FREEZES

COOLS

general title – lots of things change

the explanation

introduces second part of explanation/ diagram

'can be put back', 'can go back to what they were'

repeated in every sentence

opposites

arrows indicate direction of change

2: 2: T19: to read flow charts and cyclical diagrams that explain a process

2: 2: T21: to produce simple flow charts or diagrams that explain a process

Shuttle mission  by Ian Graham

Background

The children will probably have some knowledge of space, much of it from the fantasy of television and films. This text explores the reality, by explaining how the Space Shuttle takes off and lands. The Shuttle can fly like a rocket and like an aeroplane. The main part, *the Orbiter*, has wings like a plane. It is carried into space by rockets. *The Orbiter* carries people and equipment for experiments in space and also launches satellites. This extract provides a labelled diagram to illustrate the take-off and landing process. The technical terminology is unlikely to be a barrier in such a context. The text is written in the simple present tense, and has the feel of an eyewitness commentary. This can be compared to a recount of the same event.

What's on the CD-ROM

This version presents the labelled diagram without the written text. This will allow less able readers to explore the cyclical process. They can then use the labels to write sentences to explain the process.

Discussing the text

● Display the text and ask the class what they think it is about. Read the title and share knowledge of space and spaceships, distinguishing fact from fiction as appropriate.

● Ask the children why they think the pictures are drawn *around* the text. (To emphasises the cyclical process.) Ask the children where you should start 'reading' the pictures, noting that they are *not* read from the top, left to right.

● Starting at *take off*, discuss each picture and its label. Demonstrate syllabic segmentation to help with reading longer words.

● Consider what happens when you have read the pictures all the way round. (The Shuttle could take off again, showing that this is a cycle of events.)

● Read the text in the centre, clarifying new vocabulary. As you re-read, ask the children to match the text to the illustrations. Note that the text explains the stages of the process and that the picture labels are often abbreviated 'sentences' that also sometimes give additional information.

● Re-read the first sentence, using expression for dramatic effect. Discuss the effect of *soars* by comparing it with a more mundane alternative such as *flies* or *goes*. Develop this by asking the children to read the text to each other, or describe it in their own words, as if they were reporters at the scene, recounting events as they happen. Encourage them to use expression and changes in volume and pace to add drama.

● Together, rewrite the first two sentences in the past tense, noting that it is now a report *after* the event. Ask the children to highlight the verbs that have changed. Compare the immediacy and drama of the present tense report with the 'distance' of the past tense.

Talk, read and write

● Provide cut-out illustrations for the children to sequence as a cycle, adding arrows to reinforce the consecutive stages and the cyclical process.

● Model how to turn labels into complete sentences, adding further information from the text if appropriate. Include time connectives to emphasise the sequence of events. Now ask the children to write captions for each picture, using response partners to check their work.

● Organise small drama groups to prepare on-the-spot news reports of the mission. Encourage them to incorporate interviews with eyewitnesses or the astronauts giving their viewpoints and responses. Different groups could take different stages of the mission. If possible, watch a fuller television report to inform this. The children could then create 'after the event' reports, orally or in writing.

● Help the children to write definitions of technical vocabulary for a class glossary. Some children might use their general knowledge and other reference sources to add other related words.

Extension

Ask children to record the events of one day, perhaps at the weekend, as they happen. They should then rewrite these in the past tense as a report on what they did yesterday. Organise for these to be presented to the class, dramatising the events through the use of expression, even if nothing dramatic happens!

2: 2: T20: to make class dictionaries and glossaries of special interest words, giving explanations and definitions

2: 2: S9: to secure the use of simple sentences in own writing

object in orbit around a planet; we launch satellites for study and telecommunication

dramatic, exciting verb choice

'space travellers'

term for main part of shuttle that carries crew

layers of gas that surround a planet

dramatic, exciting verb choice

journey for a purpose; sounds exciting and adventurous; also a military term

Shuttle mission

Doors close

Doors open and satellite is launched

Rockets fire

Re-enters Earth's atmosphere

Glides back to Earth

The Space Shuttle soars into the sky from its launch pad. The booster rockets and the external fuel tank fall away when they have used up all of their fuel.

In space, the astronauts launch a satellite with the help of the Orbiter's long robot arm.

At the end of the mission, the Orbiter's rocket engines fire to slow it down, and it begins to fall back to Earth. It glows with heat as it plunges back into the air around Earth. Then it glides down and lands on a runway like a plane.

Booster rockets fall away

Boosters parachute into the sea and are used again

Shuttle takes off

In orbit

Fuel tank falls away

Text extract and illustration from "My Best Book of Spaceships" by Ian Graham © 1998, Kingfisher Publications plc

goes backwards and forwards (to space)

path of satellite or spaceship around a planet

provide added power

'on the outside'

float gently (used as verb here)

2: 2: T19: to read flow charts and cyclical diagrams that explain a process

2: 2: W5: to discriminate, orally, syllables in multi-syllabic words

2: 2: S5: to use verb tenses with increasing accuracy

Great Fire of London

by Rhoda Nottridge and by Jane Shuter, Adam Hook and Judith Maguire

Background

These two extracts present information about the Great Fire of London in different ways, encouraging comparison of the approaches. The first extract recounts the start of the fire and engages the reader through a newspaper report style. The second suggests reasons for the ignition and spread of the fire and poses questions to draw in the reader. The text introduces the question of how we know historical facts (and it is assumed that the nature of historical evidence will be considered in history lessons). This can be linked to the next extracts from Pepys' diary. The text will encourage children to consider 'fact' and 'fiction' in a historical context and to ask and answer questions, using *wh* question words.

What's on the CD-ROM

This is a shorter version of the second extract provided to help less able readers to ask and answer questions, using key question words. The sentences are generally simple and present key facts in an accessible recount style. The text can be used in guided reading to explore similar objectives related to questions and to present and past tense verb forms.

Discussing the text

● Find out what the children already know about the fire, establishing it as an event that happened a long time in the past. Read the first extract and ask the children to tell their partners, in their own words, what it told them.

● Re-read the title and consider the dramatic effect of the present tense, headline style, grabbing the reader's attention. Elicit that events in the past are normally retold in the past tense as the text itself is. Highlight some of the past tense verbs and ask the children what the present tense would be.

● Note the narrative features of the extract, which has similarities with stories and recounts – scene setting, which builds suspense, and a series of chronological events that focus on particular characters. Ensure that the children appreciate this extract recounts the start of a real historical event and is, therefore, non-fiction. Consider, however, that perhaps some of the details are not strictly *facts*, that some

might have been 'guessed' to increase the sense of drama (such as the *escape across the rooftops*). Refer to work in history on the nature of evidence.

● Now read the second extract (highlighting the capital letters in *The Great Fire of London*) and discuss how it differs from the first. What does this extract tell us? What does it not tell us? This extract does not mention particular people nor describe events, but simply states facts, focusing on reasons for the severity of the fire and how we know these details.

Talk, read and write

● In guided reading, focus on the use of questions. Read the first sentence of the first extract and ask what questions would have given these answers – *When did the fire happen?* and *Where...?* Write down these questions. Repeat for other statements and then ask pairs to identify other questions, using both extracts, such as: *How did the fire start? Why did it spread?* Ask the pairs to write down their questions and the answers, as a way of summarising what they have learned from the extracts.

● Ask a group to list question words and to create large posters for reference in the classroom.

● Ask the children to identify past tense verbs in the extracts and sort them into regular (*-ed*) and irregular forms, with their partners. Some children could be given appropriate pairs to match. Give children other present tense verbs to explore, using dictionaries if appropriate. These could be made into spelling posters for the classroom.

Extension

Give children a list of question words and ask them to write one question using each, about a particular topic, and then to answer it. This might be a current class topic or one of children's own interests.

2: 3: T14: to pose questions and record these in writing, prior to reading non-fiction to find answers

past tense of 'to burn'

such an important event it has been given capital letters

question draws in reader

past tense of to 'fight'

an eyewitness on-the-spot account

2: 3: S6: to turn statements into questions

fires were not unusual

after a long, hot summer

using evidence to answer question

Extract 2

FIRE!

The Great Fire of London started on 2 September 1666, in Pudding Lane. Fires often happened in Tudor and Stuart times. Open fires were used for heating and cooking. Candles were used for lights. Accidents were likely with all these flames about. What was surprising about the Great Fire was how fast it spread, and how much of the city it burnt. Why was it such a bad fire?

To answer this question we have to look at the way that people fought fires at the time. We also need to look at how London was built. We are lucky to have the diary of Samuel Pepys, who was in London during the fire. He wrote down the things he saw and heard. This should give us some clues.

Text extract from "Our World: Tudor and Stuart Times" by Jane Shuter, Adam Hook and Judith Maguire © 1992, Jane Shuter, Adam Hook and Judith Maguire (1992, Heinemann Educational); photo © Csaba Polgar

like a newspaper headline; present tense gives sense of immediacy (rest of text is past tense, as in a newspaper report)

sets scene

where

what

when

why

past tense of 'begin'

how

what the neighbours shouted; more drama; exclamation marks for emphasis and urgency

past tense of 'blow'

how and why fire spread

how do we know? some guesswork and interpretation

repetition adds to dramatic pace of events

Extract 1

A BAKERY BURNS DOWN

A year after the plague, London had a long, hot summer. The wooden buildings were as dry as firewood. It would only take a few sparks of fire to set a house alight.

Those sparks began in a bakery in Pudding Lane. The baker and his family and servants were asleep upstairs. In the bakery below, the dry wood kept to stoke the ovens caught fire. Soon flames were spreading through the building.

FIRE! FIRE!

The baker's family was awoken by neighbours and escaped from the fire by climbing across the roof to the next building. Everyone tried to put out the fire with buckets of water. By dawn, fire was spreading faster and faster. A strong wind blew the flames from house to house, across dozens of houses were on fire. A strong wind blew the flames from house to house, across the very narrow streets.

Text extract from "Beginning History: Plagueland Fire" by Rhoda Nottridge © 1990, Wayland (Publishers) Limited

2: 3: T13: to understand the distinction between fact and fiction

2: 3: T16: to scan a text to find specific sections

2: 3: S3: to use standard forms of verbs in speaking and writing

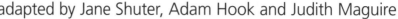

The diary of Samuel Pepys

adapted by Jane Shuter, Adam Hook and Judith Maguire

Background

These extracts follow on from the previous ones on the Great Fire of London and address the key historical question about the events – How do we know? The text allows children to explore the personal nature of diaries and the significance of this famous one. Children might note that Pepys must have been an important man if he could speak directly to the King and the Lord Mayor! The diary contains a mixture of tenses and styles, giving different effects that can be explored, and prompts further consideration of the difference between fact and fiction. The information can be reorganised under subheadings that can be used to pose questions. Children can then scan the text for key words to answer their questions.

What's on the CD-ROM

Key points from the diary extracts are rewritten here in more basic language. In guided reading, children can again pose questions to focus their interaction with the text and can organise information according to the questions posed.

Discussing the text

● Read the title and remind the children that Samuel Pepys was a real person who lived in London at the time of the Great Fire. First, encourage the children to share their experiences of using diaries. What do they write about? Then return to the text and ask: *Will Pepys' diary contain facts or fiction?* You might introduce the term *opinion*, since diaries contain a writer's personal thoughts and interpretations (although these extracts focus on facts on the whole). Explain that Pepys wrote the diary for himself, not knowing that it would be so valuable in the future.

● Read the extracts, pinning down the chronological order of events and the time span covered. Help with unfamiliar vocabulary and grammar as necessary. Then ask pairs to tell each other two or three things that Pepys reveals about the fire.

● Look for features that show that this is a personal eyewitness account, for example the use of *I*, the words of the Lord Mayor (in speech marks) and phrases such as *With your face in the wind…* and *Going to the fire…*

● Highlight the verbs in the first extract.

Revise the difference between past and present tense verbs and consider the effect of immediacy generated with the present tense. Ask the children to imagine Pepys going out into the streets during the day and writing his diary at home in the evening. What he saw is reported in the past tense and what is still happening is in the present.

● Re-read the final extract and ask the children to explain how the fire was stopped. Notice the more positive tone that Pepys uses at this point.

Talk, read and write

● Ask the children to share what they learned from Pepys' diary. Gather these key points on the board and ask for suggestions on how to group them. (If this is done in a later session the points can be printed or written onto strips and cut up for children to organise.) Possible groupings are: *why the fire spread, what people did during the fire, how the fire was stopped*. Group the ideas accordingly and add subheadings.

● Now take each subheading and model how to turn it into a question. Then, using one question, model how to scan each extract, highlighting key words and phrases that relate to that question. Ask the children to continue on their own copies, ideally in mixed-ability pairs.

● Use guided writing to convert the highlighted words or phrases into a sentence that answers the question. For example, in response to *Why did the fire spread so quickly?* the answer *After so long without rain* can become *The fire spread quickly because there had been no rain for a long time*.

● Some children could combine answers from the diary extracts and the previous text to write a fuller report of the Great Fire to present to the class.

● Give pairs cloze copies of the text for completion.

Extension

Encourage children to write diary entries for a week, remembering to write in the first person and considering details that might bring the entries alive for a reader, such as their thoughts at particular points.

2: 3: T14: to pose questions and record these in writing, prior to reading non-fiction to find answers

2: 3: S6: to turn statements into questions

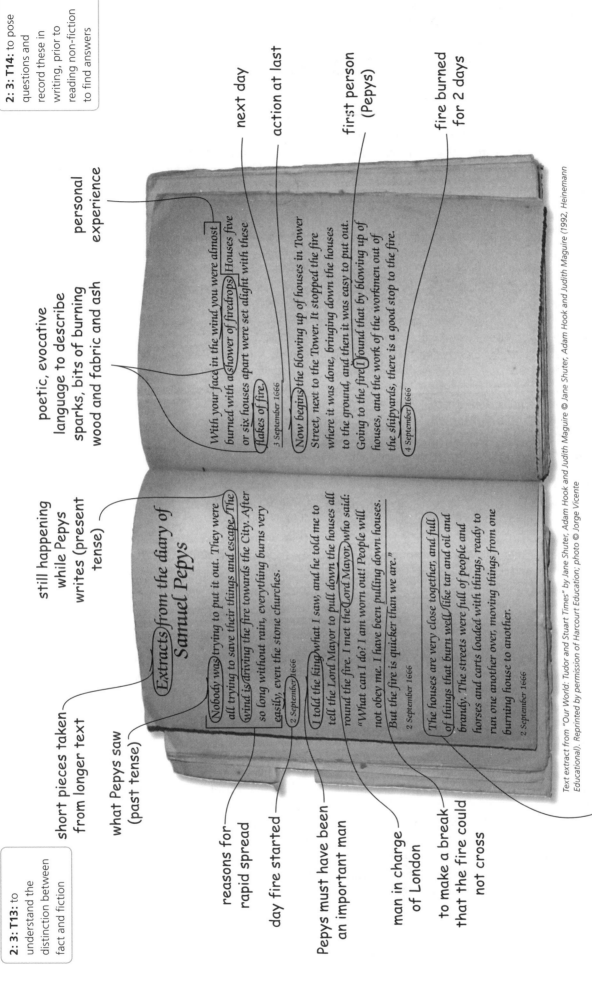

next day

action at last

first person (Pepys)

fire burned for 2 days

personal experience

poetic, evocative language to describe sparks, bits of burning wood and fabric and ash

still happening while Pepys writes (present tense)

chronological order of events

Extracts from the diary of Samuel Pepys

With your face in the wind you were almost burned with a shower of firedrops. Houses five or six houses apart were set alight with these flakes of fire.
3 September 1666

Now begins the blowing up of houses in Tower Street, next to the Tower. It stopped the fire where it was done, bringing down the houses to the ground, and then it was easy to put out. Going to the fire I found that by blowing up of houses, and the work of the workmen out of the shipyards, there is a good stop to the fire.
4 September 1666

Nobody was trying to put it out. They were all trying to save their things and escape. The wind is driving the fire towards the City. After so long without rain, everything burns very easily, even the stone churches.
2 September 1666

I told the king what I saw, and he told me to tell the Lord Mayor to pull down the houses all round the fire. I met the Lord Mayor, who said: "What can I do? I am worn out! People will not obey me. I have been pulling down houses. But the fire is quicker than we are."
2 September 1666

The houses are very close together, and full of things that burn well (like tar and oil and brandy. The streets were full of people and horses and carts loaded with things, ready to run one another over, moving things from one burning house to another.
2 September 1666

short pieces taken from longer text

what Pepys saw (past tense)

reasons for rapid spread

day fire started

Pepys must have been an important man

man in charge of London

to make a break that the fire could not cross

more reasons for spread

Text extract from "Our World: Tudor and Stuart Times" by Jane Shuter, Adam Hook and Judith Maguire © Jane Shuter, Adam Hook and Judith Maguire (1992, Heinemann Educational). Reprinted by permission of Harcourt Education; photo © Jorge Vicente

2: 3: T13: to understand the distinction between fact and fiction

2: 3: T16: to scan a text to find specific sections

Book blurb — elephants by Will Travers

Background

Will Travers is the son of Bill Travers and Virginia McKenna, stars of the 1964 film *Born Free*, about the conservation work of George and Joy Adamson in Africa. The couple were so affected by the issues in the film that they devoted much of their lives to similar causes. The family launched the Born Free Foundation in 1991, to coordinate a number of wildlife projects. This extract is the blurb and author information from the book that provides the following extract, 'Meet the elephant', page 84. The text offers the opportunity to consider the distinction between fact and fiction and between fiction and non-fiction texts. It can also be used to develop awareness of authorship and publication and to consider the purpose of a book blurb.

What's on the CD-ROM

This simplified version will enable less able readers to engage with a book blurb and read about the author and so meet similar objectives to others. The language is simplified, but key details of the book contents and the author's 'credentials' are retained. The text could be used in guided group work on fiction and non-fiction texts and as a starting point for children's own biographies.

Discussing the text

● Before reading the text, check the children's understanding of *fact* and *fiction*. Ask them to suggest facts, such as *Today is Tuesday*. Then give them some statements and ask whether they are fact or fiction, such as *X [child in class] has long hair; Rapunzel had long hair that reached to the bottom of her tower.* You might introduce examples of *opinion* or *possibility*, which are neither fact nor fiction, such as *Long hair is nicer than short hair; Tomorrow it might rain.*

● Use some familiar classroom books to establish which are fiction and which contain facts, using the term *non-fiction*. It might be appropriate to include a book about a historical character or a biography, which present facts in narrative style.

● Read the blurb, explaining vocabulary where necessary. Ask: *Where in a book would you find this kind of writing?* Use the term *blurb* and establish the purpose of such information (to make someone want to read the book). *Who writes blurbs?* Explain the role of a publisher in producing and marketing a book.

● Ask whether this blurb is from a fiction or a non-fiction book and how we can tell. Note the initial focus on a particular elephant calf, but draw attention to the generic title, *Elephant,* the technical vocabulary and the later sentences, which extend the focus to elephants in general.

● Note how the direct language (*Follow, Join, Meet*) and the focus on an individual calf engage the reader by creating the effect of a personal encounter. Ask the children if the blurb has been successful – do they want to find out more?

● Discuss why the author information is included. Note the connection between the author's experiences and the subject of the book. Discuss the purpose in listing other books in the series, to show the book's 'pedigree' and to encourage a reader to buy more books.

Talk, read and write

● Explore the author information on a range of books. Then use the first person to record some biographical information about yourself. Pose questions to elicit similar details from a child and write the answers on the board, using the third person, and note the differences. Now ask the children to interview each other and write biographies (noting that these are 'true stories', non-fiction). Questions could first be generated as a class and a writing frame could support independent writing.

● Ask groups to sort a range of books into fiction and non-fiction, perhaps including biographies. Then ask them to select blurbs to read to the rest of the class. The class should then decide whether they are from fiction or non-fiction and vote on which book they most want to read.

● Ask pairs to note questions they would like to ask about elephants, for use with the following extract.

Extension

Ask children to choose a favourite book – fiction or non-fiction – and write a blurb for it.

2: 3: T13: to understand the distinction between fact and fiction

2: 3: T18: to evaluate the usefulness of a text for its purpose

refer to factual information inside this non-fiction book

intial focus on a particular elephant calf

focus extended to elephants in general

the informative text on a book cover is the 'blurb'

Page from "Natural World – Elephant" by Will Travers © 1999, Wayland (Publishers) Ltd, by permission of Hodder and Stoughton Limited

NATURAL WORLD

WAYLAND

ELEPHANT

Follow an elephant calf as it takes its first steps on its exciting journey through life in the African savannah.

Join the calf as it explores its surroundings, and watch it learn the skills it needs from the other members of the elephant herd.

• Meet some of the other animals that share the elephants' watering hole.

• Find out about the threats facing elephants in Africa and in Asia and what can be done to protect these amazing creatures.

The author **Will Travers** has dedicated most of his life to wildlife and animal issues. He is co-founder and Chief Executive of the Born Free Foundation, a charitable organization that cares for wild animals. Its projects span five continents and include the rescue, conservation and protection of elephants, chimpanzees and big cats.

Other animals to meet in the **Natural World** series include:

CHIMPANZEE • GIANT PANDA • GREAT WHITE SHARK
KILLER WHALE • LION • POLAR BEAR • TIGER

WAYLAND

£10.99

ISBN 0-590-55825-0

generic title (in large, capital letters) makes subject of book clear

imperatives – direct language engages the reader

technical vocabulary

photo of the author adds interest

other books in the series listed to encourage the reader to buy them

publisher

suggested price

2: 3: S6: to turn statements into questions

2: 3: T5: to read about authors from information book covers

Meet the elephant
by Will Travers

Background
This extract is from the same non-fiction book as the blurb on page 82. Moving from the general to the specific in its information about elephants, it focuses on differences between the two species, from which children can make notes and organise information. It also allows exploration of the language used for comparison, including conjunctions and comparative adjectives. The meaningful context will enable children to engage with unfamiliar language, and a map and illustrations add visual support to the written text.

What's on the CD-ROM
This writing frame provides a structure for a non-chronological report comparing the two species of elephant. It provides appropriate sentence starters and connectives, and employs the contrastive conjunction *while*. With support in guided groups, children will be able to identify key information about the two types of elephant from the core text and use this frame to construct a cohesive text.

Discussing the text
● If relevant, remind the children about the previous text, and explain that this is an extract from Will Travers' book. Remind them of their questions (see Talk, read and write on page 82), which will provide a focus for reading.

● Read the title, noting how it addresses and engages the reader, and adopts the language of the blurb.

● Read the first two paragraphs, which provide general facts about elephants and emphasise their amazing qualities, again drawing in the reader. Ask children to highlight key words and phrases.

● Read the caption about habitats, explaining unfamiliar vocabulary as necessary. Explore the map, guiding use of the key, and notice that the elephant species are named after the two continents on which they are found. (Note that *savannah* is an African feature, whereas the others may be found on either continent.) Again ask volunteers to highlight key words and phrases.

● Read the next paragraph, explaining the term *species* and the Latin classifications. Note connections with familiar words: *maximus* –

maximum; *Loxodonta* – dental.) Emphasise the balanced structure of the last sentence, with *but* separating opposing clauses.

● Read the rest of the text, then ask the class to identify key features that distinguish African and Asian elephants. Note particularly the language used to make comparisons – the use of *while* as a conjunction and comparative adjectives such as *taller, rougher.*

● Find out if any of the questions generated in the previous session have been answered by this text. If not, discuss other sources of information, to be explored later.

Talk, read and write
● In guided groups, ask the children to suggest a subheading for each section. Use the key points highlighted earlier as prompts. For example, the introductory paragraphs might be entitled *What makes elephants special?* Add these to the text and note how the text moves from *general* information about all elephants to *specific* features that distinguish the species.

● Prepare a table with a column for each species, and a row for each subheading. Model and then ask the children to transfer the suggested subheadings using key words. If necessary, explore antonyms to help the children understand comparative adjectives. Show that the information from the introductory sections can be put in both columns because these are the similarities between the two species. If using ICT, children could merge cells to show this.

● Ask the children to research further information, adapting their earlier questions as row headings, under general or species-specific sections.

● The same model might be used to research and present information on other animal 'pairs', such as butterflies/moths, crocodiles/alligators.

● You might use the writing frame on the CD-ROM to model how to turn new information into sentences, using *while* or comparative adjectives and connectives to produce cohesive text.

Extension
Using two 'types' within a familiar topic, ask children to complete another table of similarities and differences.

general facts about elephants

key aids understanding of map

Latin classifications

balanced sentence with 'but' separating opposing clauses

Meet the elephant

Elephants are the largest land animals in the world. They are very strong, extremely intelligent and have remarkable memories.

Unlike most animals, elephants continue to grow throughout their lives – the older they get, the bigger and more impressive they are.

Elephants live in many different habitats, including savannah, rainforests, swamps and mountains.

Key to map
African elephants
Asian elephants

There are two species of elephant. They are the Asian elephant (*Elephas maximus*) and the African elephant (*Loxodonta Africana*). They may look very similar, but there are important differences.

African elephants weigh between 4–7 tonnes, while Asian elephants weigh between 3–5 tonnes. At up to 4 metres high, the African elephant is also about a metre taller than the Asian elephant.

The tusks of an African elephant are bigger than those of the Asian elephant and its ears are also bigger. African elephants normally have rougher, more wrinkled skin than Asian elephants.

African elephant

Text extract, map and illustration from "Natural World – Elephant" by Will Travers; text © 1999, Will Travers (1999, Wayland Publishers Ltd)

imperative structure of title addresses and engages the reader

amazing qualities of elephants emphasised

type

differences between the two species highlighted

comparative adjectives

Reptiles of long ago by Scholastic Ltd

Background

Most children are fascinated by dinosaurs and many will know something about them already. Some of this may have been learned from films, such as *Jurassic Park*, so this text helps in distinguishing fact from fiction. The extract comes from an encyclopedia section on amphibians and reptiles (hence the title). There is an introductory paragraph and several sections under subheadings, with a captioned photograph of a model. Children can pose questions and develop skills of skimming and scanning for key information. Although some of the vocabulary is difficult, children's interest should make the text accessible, and it offers a meaningful opportunity to reinforce use of syllabification for reading. Although many non-fiction texts make use of the present tense, facts about dinosaurs are of course written in the past tense.

What's on the CD-ROM

This version gives similar information but more briefly and with simpler sentence structures. It is organised under subheadings to allow less able readers to develop skimming skills.

Discussing the text

● Reveal just the title and picture and ask what the text is about. Then ask the children to brainstorm in groups, before sharing with the class, everything they know about dinosaurs.

● Ask whether this text will be fiction or non-fiction. Draw a distinction between facts (derived from evidence) and fictional film interpretations (which might, however, be *based* on facts). Note that the picture shows a model, based on evidence. Ask: *Why do we have no photographs of dinosaurs?*

● Re-read the title and ask the children to suggest why it is not 'Dinosaurs'. The text begins by discussing reptiles in general, of which dinosaurs were one type, now extinct.

● Read the introduction and discuss the issues raised, noting that dinosaurs were on Earth for a very long time. Some children might know of the theories about why they disappeared, such as changes in climate or habitats, or meteor impact.

● Reveal the rest of the text and point out its organisation in sections. Elicit the purpose of the introduction providing general background information and 'setting the scene'.

● Read the subheadings and ask the children what they expect to learn from the text. Model how to turn some of the subheadings into questions, for example *What did dinosaurs eat?*

● Read each section in turn. For each section ask the children to pick out and summarise key points. Prompt discussions on, for example: why modern animals are used as comparisons; what forms different dinosaurs took; how we know about dinosaurs.

Talk, read and write

● Provide reference sources for the children to research further information about particular dinosaurs.

● Tell the children they are going to make dinosaur fact files. Organise mixed-ability pairs and ask them to look for different dinosaur names. Then ask them to list these as the first column of a table. Suggest topics for other column headings, use information from the class text to suggest headings such as *how many legs did they walk on.* Tell the children to find key information about each dinosaur and transfer this to their fact file tables. Remind them that full sentences are not needed for this kind of presentation (*only leaves*, for example, under a column heading of *food*).

● Ask the children if there are any further questions they want to ask about dinosaurs. Tell them to decide first whether they think this text will contain the answer, then scan the text for the key words.

Extension

Ask the children to compile fact files about themselves and/or family or friends. Some children might need a writing frame or chart with headings such as name, age, height, hair/ eye colour, favourite food. Suggest the type of questions they could ask to establish information: *How old are you? What is your favourite colour?* Remind them that they do not need to answer with full sentences.

2: 3: T16: to scan a text to find specific sections

2: 3: T17: to skim read illustrations, chapter headings and subheadings to speculate what a book might be about

model in photo is an interpretation, based on evidence

size comparisons using familiar things to aid understanding

information organised under subheadings

2: 3: T19: to make simple notes from non-fiction texts to use in subsequent writing

Text © 2007, Scholastic Ltd; photo © Fotoredaction drs, online

REPTILES
of long ago

From 260 million years ago until around 65 million years ago is known as the Age of Reptiles. During that time, reptiles were the most successful animals on Earth. Some kinds of reptiles that were alive then still exist today, such as crocodiles. Others, such as dinosaurs, died out suddenly. Nobody knows exactly why. We can find out about dinosaurs from their fossils.

There were many different kinds of dinosaurs. They were reptiles, like the lizards and snakes that are alive today.

ALL SHAPES...

Dinosaurs came in a wide variety of shapes. Some dinosaurs walked slowly on four legs. They had long necks and tails which they held out to help them balance. Others ran on two legs as ostriches do today. Some dinosaurs had bony plates and sails on their back to help them warm up and cool down. Many had vicious spikes, spines and horns on their bodies or heads to attack enemies with.

...AND SIZES

The biggest dinosaurs were the sauropods. They had long necks and tails and the largest were nearly 20 metres tall. They could weigh as much as sixty small cars. The smallest dinosaurs were tiny by comparison. Some were only the size of chickens.

DINOSAUR FOOD

Many dinosaurs ate plants. They had many tiny teeth designed for chewy food. They didn't need to move fast to catch their food. However, the smaller ones had to move fast to get away from meat-eating dinosaurs. The meat-eaters had fearsome, shapr teeth, perfect for tearing flesh. Some had terrible claws for slashing their prey.

introductory paragraph sets the scene

text begins by discussing reptiles in general (of which dinosaurs were one type)

suggests that there are different theories

linked subheadings

2: 3: T13: to understand the distinction between fact and fiction

2: 3: T14: to pose questions and record these in writing prior to reading non-fiction to find answers

2: 3: W2: to reinforce work on discriminating syllables in reading and spelling from previous term

Solar System — contents and index

by Stephanie Turnbull

Background

These contents and index pages are from a non-fiction book about the Solar System. They will reinforce understanding of how non-fiction differs from fiction and provide useful revision of ways to locate information. Children are likely to have some knowledge of space and can develop their ideas and vocabulary in a meaningful context. These extracts can be used in conjunction with the following text extract from a book on the same subject.

What's on the CD-ROM

The same contents and index are presented here in reduced form. They include only items specifically related to objects in the Solar System. The index has been organised so that items beginning with the same letter are grouped, enabling children to grasp the alphabetical nature of an index without having to engage with more than first-letter ordering.

Discussing the text

● If possible, have a range of relevant non-fiction and fiction texts on display. Before reading this text, discuss the differences between fiction and non-fiction. Ask the children to categorise the books on display and say how they know which is which. Ask: *What would you expect to find in each type of book?* Note that non-fiction texts often contain *facts*, but may also embellish or speculate about events or present different points of view (such as the reasons for dinosaurs dying out).

● Now read the two titles and establish understanding of the terms. *Where would you find a contents and an index? What are they for?*

● Show the contents and index in other non-fiction books, noting their positions near the front and the back. You might show some fiction books that have a contents list of chapters but never an index.

● Read the *Contents* list and ask what the book it came from is likely to be about. Check understanding of terminology, noting where capital letters are used for names. Discuss the purpose and organisation of a glossary (to be found on page 30). Note how some titles are not self-explanatory, such as *Vanishing Trick*, and that the sense of mystery might draw a

reader to that page.

● Ask the children how a reader might use a contents list, and confirm by modelling how to skim the headings to find a certain item. (You might need to clarify what is on page 5 or 7.)

● Now read the *Index*, or part of it, and ask the children whether they think it is from the same book. Ask what order this list is in and how a reader would use it. It is a list of key words in the book. A particular word might be found on more than one page (for example *astronauts* appears on four pages: *18, 19, 29, 30*). An entry such as *14–15* indicates a longer *continuous* reference (over two pages).

● Model how to cross-reference contents and index entries. For example, a reader wanting to find out about the Moon would find just one chapter heading in the contents list. The index, however, indicates other references, which can be checked against the chapter headings to establish, for example, that *A rocky desert* is also about the Moon.

Talk, read and write

● Set questions about the extracts that require either straight information retrieval or cross-referencing. For example: *On which pages would you find references to Mars? Is Mars a nearby or a faraway planet?* Then challenge the children to set their own questions for others to answer.

● Let the children pose questions about the Solar System that they would like to find answers to. Ask them to skim the contents and then scan the index to determine whether this book would help. If available, let them extend their research to other books.

● Hand out a selection of non-fiction texts on this topic or another being studied. Ask the children to record on reference cards the book titles and whether they have a contents, index or glossary.

Extension

Children could compile the contents and index for a non-fiction book on a familiar subject. This could be linked to the *Did you know…?* books suggested as an extension for the next text.

2: 3: T17: to skim read contents page to speculate what a book might be about

surface holes and dents made by meteors

to do with the moon

2 names for same phenomenon

capital letters for named planets or bodies

2: 3: T18: to evaluate the usefulness of a text for its purpose

several pages include information on this topic

alphabetical order

Index

Contents

Contents and index from "Usborne Beginners: Sun, Moon and Stars" by Stephanie Turnbull © 2003, Usborne Publishing Ltd; photo © Maciej Ciupa

2: 3: T13: to understand the distinction between fact and fiction

2: 3: T15: to use contents page and index to find way about text

page numbers in numerical order

planets divided into two groups

what might this mean? (solar eclipse)

constellations and galaxies

index appears at back of book

2: 3: W9: to learn new words from reading linked to particular topics

What is the sun? by Jillian Powell

Background

This extract is an introduction to the Sun, the centre of our Solar System and essential to life on Earth. It can be linked to the previous text – contents and index pages from a book about space and the Solar System and with work in science. The information is presented in both textual and visual ways, with subheadings and 'fact boxes'. Many children will bring knowledge to the subject and will be able to generate questions to give focus to their reading. The text offers opportunities to develop the non-fiction reading and writing skills of posing questions, scanning text and making notes.

What's on the CD-ROM

This is a simplified text about the Sun. It contains similar information to the core text, but much more briefly and using simpler sentence structures. In guided sessions less able readers will be able to generate questions and scan the text for key words and phrases to use in their own writing.

Discussing the text

● Read the title and ask the children to answer the question in pairs or small groups. Share this existing knowledge, then ask the groups to discuss what else they would like to find out. Demonstrate how to turn their suggestions into questions, focusing on the spelling of question words and the use of question marks. Ask the groups to prioritise and write down two or three questions for future use.

● Draw attention to layout features of the text, exploring the readability of short sentences dotted with fact boxes and pictures.

● Read the text, but cover the diagram. Note the huge distances and sizes, impossible to visualise. Highlight the comparatives – *bigger, smaller, brighter, closer* – that relate one thing to another. Now ask children tell a partner some facts they have learned from the text.

● Note the use of a subheading to introduce a different aspect of the topic, and an explanation. Talk about the effect of the question *Did you know...?*, noting that sometimes people use this when they want to 'show off' their knowledge.

● Reveal the diagram and re-read this section to show how the picture supports understanding. Give a practical demonstration if appropriate.

● Highlight the *ear* spelling pattern in *year* and *Earth*. Note the different pronunciation of the same letters (but emphasise that the pronunciation in *Earth* is uncommon). Brainstorm other words that rhyme with *year* and note different spelling patterns (including *eer* and *ere*). Also remind the children that *ear* can also be said 'air' as in *bear.*

Talk, read and write

● In shared writing, select one of the questions posed earlier that can be answered from the text. Pick out the key words from the question. First model how to use the layout of the text to decide where the answer might be found. Then scan the text to locate the key words. Write the answer in note form, then model the answer as a complete sentence.

● Give the children questions that can be answered from the text, reminding them of the strategies modelled in shared writing.

● Then ask the children to find and write answers to the questions they posed earlier. Make a note of those for which there is no answer in the text and encourage some children to research other reference sources. More able learners could generate additional questions for others to answer from the text.

● Give each pair of children matching sets of cards with words or phrases from the text. Ask them to compete to locate the words and read out the sentence.

● At word level, ask the children to generate, and classify by spelling, other words that contain the phoneme 'ear'. These could be made into posters for display. More able learners could focus on other words that have the spelling pattern *ear* but different sounds (in a wordsearch for example).

Extension

Ask children to compile *Did you know...?* books about a topic they are 'experts' on. Encourage them to jot down facts about their subject and then write and illustrate sentences beginning with *Did you know...* Children could give presentations on their subject and other children could prepare questions to ask them.

2: 3: T16: to scan a text to find specific sections

2: 3: T19: to make simple notes from non-fiction texts to use in subsequent writing

2: 3: T21: to write non-chronological reports based on structure on known texts

2: 3: W3: to discriminate, spell and read the phonemes 'ear' and 'ea'

title in form of question draws in reader

too far to imagine!

comparatives relate one thing to another; use 'er' ending

one whole day

text in panels catches the eye; facts don't have to be read in order

huge, incomprehensible numbers

technical term for the way heat and light travels

plants and animals

spelling pattern with different sounds

we often open questions like this when talking to each other; anticipates surprise

difficult to understand fully without diagram

2: 3: T14: to pose questions and record these in writing, prior to reading non-fiction to find answers

2: 3: T18: to evaluate the usefulness of a text for its purpose

2: 3: T20: to write non-fiction texts, using texts read as models for own writing

What is the sun?

The Sun is a star. It is shining far out in space, 150 million kilometres away.

The Sun is more than a million times bigger than the Earth. It seems smaller because it is so far away.

The Sun looks brighter than other stars because it is closer to the Earth than they are.

The Sun is billions of years old. The Sun that shone on the dinosaurs is the same one that shines on us today.

The Sun's rays give us light and warmth. We call its light daylight.

We can only see the Sun during the day.

Everything on the Earth needs sunshine to live and to grow.

The Earth spins round once every 24 hours

Sun fact
The Earth travels round the Sun. It takes just over one year to go right round.

Sun fact
The light from the Sun makes the Moon shine.

Day and night
We call the start of the day **sunrise** and the end of the day **sunset**.

The Sun is often a lovely colour at these times.

Did you know the Sun is shining all the time, even when you can't see it?

When we have night, the Sun is shining on the other side of the world.

This is because the Earth is spinning as it travels round the Sun.

On the side of the Earth facing the Sun it is daytime. On the side facing away, the Earth is in darkness and it is night.

Text extract from "Sun and Us" by Jillian Powell © 1998, Belitha Press (1998, Anova Books); photos: sun left © Lori Morris, sun right © Cheryl Empey, sun fact © Chris Watk

Magnets

by Sue Taylor

Background

The power of magnets to make things move without touching them can be fascinating to young children. This text would be most valuable if linked to practical science investigations and observations, exploring materials and forces. It offers simple definitions and explanations of concepts, making use of key subject-specific vocabulary. The text offers the opportunity to explore features of non-chronological report, including the use of subheadings and labelled illustrations. Children can develop key non-fiction reading and writing skills of posing questions, skimming and scanning to locate answers, making notes and communicating information.

What's on the CD-ROM

A simplified version of similar information is provided. Although key vocabulary is retained, facts and concepts are explained in simpler sentences. The illustrations are retained to support the written text. The text can be used in guided reading for similar objectives of scanning text to identify key ideas and note making. Children could communicate their understanding through labelled pictures with captions or using a writing frame or grid.

Discussing the text

● Read the title and establish understanding of magnets, drawing on work in science if appropriate. Read the introductory paragraph and ask children to discuss their own experience of the uses of magnets. (They could be asked to investigate uses of magnets at home and in school as part of work in science.) Read the subheadings, noting that these give the reader an idea of what the text will be about.

● Ask children to talk to a partner about what they know and suggest things they would like to find out. Write some suggestions on the board as questions, including at least one that can be answered from the text.

● Read the subheadings and discuss the pictures, clarifying understanding of terminology where necessary. Ask children whether they think the questions posed are likely to be answered in this text, based on the subheadings.

● Read each section, again checking understanding of ideas and vocabulary (and noting that non-fiction texts commonly have a lot of vocabulary related specifically to the topic). Note the relationship between magnet, magnetism and magnetic, and the opposites attract and repel.

● After each section, ask children to summarise to a partner two or three key ideas in that section. Note how the illustrations support understanding and relate closely to the written text.

● Note the structure of the text, considering how it moves from a general introduction to the topic onto more specific information: beginning with what magnets are, what they look like and how they are used (providing a real life context) then describing specific features of their properties.

Talk, read and write

● Choose one of the questions posed earlier that can be answered from the text. Highlight key words in the question. First model how to skim the subheadings and illustrations to decide where the answer might be found. Then scan the relevant section to identify key words. Write the answer in note form and then model how to turn it into a sentence.

● Ask children to work in pairs, choosing another question, and use the same strategies to find answers. If appropriate, children could be given other books on the topic to further develop these non-fiction reading strategies, including use of contents, index and glossary.

● After practical investigations in science, children can present findings to the class, using a 'talking frame' to plan the structure of their talk and the key ideas to be included.

● Children can write definitions and explanations of technical vocabulary for individual or class glossaries or display.

Extension

Give children a wordsearch of topic words, differentiated as appropriate. When found, children can practise spelling using Look-Say-Cover-Write-Check or similar strategy. Meanings of words can be illustrated using labelled diagrams, or by using them in sentences.

2: 3: T17: to skim-read illustrations, chapter headings and subheadings, to speculate what a text might be about

2: 3: W9: to learn new words from reading linked to particular topics

illustrations support text

visually represents description given in text; use to aid understanding

Magnets

Magnets are objects which can attract certain other objects without touching them. Magnets come in different shapes. They can be curved, like horseshoes, or shaped like a bar, a ring or a cylinder. Magnets are used in lots of ways around the home. We can use magnets to stick notes to the fridge and to keep doors shut. They are sometimes used to link the carriages of toy trains and in other toys and games. Very powerful magnets are used to sort different materials for recycling.

Magnetic materials

Magnets only attract objects that contain certain materials, called magnetic materials. The metal iron is the most common magnetic material.

Magnetism

Magnetic materials are attracted to a magnet by a force called magnetism. This force can pass through some materials. A pin on a piece of paper will be attracted to a magnet on the other side of the paper. The magnet can make the pin move without touching it.

Magnetic poles

Every magnet has two poles at opposite parts or ends. These are called the north pole and the south pole. They are sometimes labelled N and S. The south pole may be painted blue and the north pole red. The north pole on one magnet will attract the south pole on another magnet. Two north poles or two south poles will repel each other.

subheadings

adjective from 'magnet'

but some can be made of other materials

scientific vocabulary

2: 3: T16: to scan a text to find specific sections

2: 3: T18: to evaluate the usefulness of a text for its purpose

The Smith family in 2005
by Scholastic Ltd

Background
This extract and the one following are best used together to explore seaside holidays today and in the past, appropriate to history and geography topics. The picture is full of information, providing opportunities to develop visual literacy. The written text, organised into three sections, describes some aspects of the picture and gives supplementary information about holidays at home and abroad. The text prompts consideration of the distinction between fact and fiction and the extension of familiar topic-related vocabulary. Children will be able to write non-chronological reports and, if used with the following extract, write comparisons. There are many opportunities for discussion and role play.

What's on the CD-ROM
In the differentiated text, the majority of the information is presented through the illustrations, but the general information is included in text form. Less able readers can look closely at the pictures and captions and extract information, making notes and developing vocabulary.

Discussing the text
● Read the title and discuss the picture. Identify family members, making comparison to the children's own families if appropriate. Ask the children whether they think this text will be fiction or non-fiction (and ask this question again later).

● Examine the picture thoroughly. Ask the children to name and describe what they see and allow plenty of talk about their own experiences of holidays or the seaside. Children who have never been to the seaside or on holiday may need extra support and resources. Prompt with questions about clothes, activities, food, items being used, seaside features.

● List key vocabulary, checking spellings where appropriate and revising compound words such as *armbands* and *suntan*.

● Read the first three paragraphs and note how they describe parts of the picture, rather like an extended caption. Pick out any further key vocabulary for your list. Help the children to understand the difference between labels (words with lines) and captions (descriptive longer phrases or sentences).

● Read the final paragraph, allowing children to discuss and compare their own experiences. Note again vocabulary specific to holidays. Ask children to summarise the content of this paragraph and suggest a subheading.

● Compare the style of the first paragraphs – describing a particular family on holiday, using names, making the text seem personal – with the final one – impersonal, giving information about holidays *in general*. Ensure that children understand that this is a non-fiction text, giving information about typical holidays, using a named family as an example.

Talk, read and write
● Hand out copies of the list of vocabulary compiled earlier (ideally cut up into separate words/phrases) and ask the children to sort them into titled groups. These could be expressed as statements (such as *What people are wearing*) or simpler labels (*Clothes*). Ask the children to write each title and its words into separate boxes on a page or into a table.

● In shared writing, use this information to write a non-chronological report, with a title, an introductory sentence and subheadings (using their box titles). Model how to turn the list of words into sentences. Ask the children to continue the report independently, with some using a writing frame or working in a guided group. Alternatively, this activity could be adapted as a comparison task after studying the next extract.

● In small groups, ask the children to role play seaside activities, to develop their use of vocabulary. These could be done initially as freeze-frames for others to guess the activity, before moving into a more complete role play. Help children who have no experience of the seaside to choose another leisure activity.

Extension
Ask children to draw and label a picture of themselves and families or carers on holiday or a day trip. Children with no experience might choose another fun activity. Some children could present these to the class.

Ask children to find out from families what holidays were like when they were young.

2: 3: T19: to make simple notes from non-fiction texts to use in subsequent writing

2: 3: T20: to write non-fiction texts, using texts read as models for own writing

everyday topic words

general information about seaside holidays, not just about Smith family

The Smith family in 2005

The Smiths have gone on holiday to Greece for two weeks. They like beaches and water sports.

Adam is six years old. He is learning to swim using armbands. Megan is eight. She is playing on the beach. Their dad (Steve) is taking pictures of them with his digital camera.

Mum (Jenny) is calling to the children. She wants them to put suntan lotion so they don't get burnt.

Today lots of people go abroad on holiday, to hot sunny beaches. They fly or take ferries to get there. While they are there they stay in hotels or apartments.

Text © 2007, Scholastic Ltd; illustration © Jane Bottomley

title works as caption to picture

picture contains lots of information

describes some things shown in picture

particular

general

not just 'this day', but 'in modern times' in general

...because the UK is an island

2: 3: T13: to understand the distinction between fact and fiction

2: 3: T21: to write non-chronological reports based on structure of known texts

The Watson family in 1905 by Scholastic Ltd

Background

This text can be used to explore seaside holidays in the past, and if used with the previous one, 'The Smith family in 2005', to compare with holidays today. Visual literacy will be developed through the picture, which provide most of the information. The written text supports the picture and gives additional historical information about trips to the seaside in Victorian times. Children can develop vocabulary related to the topic and in particular period-specific seaside terms, and also words related to the passing of time.

What's on the CD-ROM

The differentiated text provides the same visual information, enabling children to discuss features of Victorian seaside holidays with appropriate vocabulary but fewer reading demands. The general information, unavailable in the picture, is retained.

Discussing the text

● Cover the main text initially. Read the title, putting the date into context (for example, *more than 100 years ago*; *in the time of Queen Victoria; when your great great grandparents were alive*). Talk about the family in the picture. Do the children think this is a modern family? How do they know?

● If relevant, ask the children to share what they know about holidays when their families/ carers were young. Then ask what else they would like to know about holidays in the past. Work together to turn the ideas into questions.

● Discuss the seaside picture, without text at this stage. Ask children to describe what they see, noting that it depicts a *typical* family on holiday in 1900. Ask them to compare it with their experiences of the seaside (and the previous text if relevant). List similarities and differences, using appropriate period-specific vocabulary, such as *water wings*.

● Now read the written text and point out that it gives information about seaside holidays in 1900 in different ways. The first two paragraphs describe aspects of the picture, referring to the individuals by name, allowing the reader to engage with the information in a personal way. The second two give facts about Victorian seaside holidays in general. Note that the first section is in the present tense – describing the picture, as it *is*, and the second section is in the past tense – giving information about holidays as they *were*.

● Does the picture or written text provide answers to any of the questions generated earlier in the lesson? If not, discuss alternative sources of information, such as other non-fiction texts about holidays in the past or the internet.

Talk, read and write

● Return to the information gathered from the previous text, if relevant, and ask the children to sort information from this text in a similar way. This can be recorded on a chart, under headings such as *Clothes* and *Activities*. If being used with the previous text, this can be done in the form of a comparison chart with three columns: the feature being considered, modern-day characteristics, Victorian characteristics.

● In shared writing, develop the chart as a non-chronological report, using the feature headings as subheadings or paragraphs. If appropriate, compare modern and Victorian characteristics in each section.

● The children can complete reports independently, with guided group support or writing frames as appropriate. Encourage them to include a title and introductory sentence or paragraph.

● In groups, ask the children to prepare role plays of a day at the seaside. They can choose modern or Victorian times and ask others to guess what the activity is and when it is taking place. Alternatively they could role play both eras to demonstrate the differences.

Extension

Give children sets of topic-related vocabulary to sort into *modern* or *Victorian*, or *both*. They could then draw and label two pictures to illustrate the vocabulary. Alternatively, ask children to draw and label a holiday or leisure activity remembered by an adult and make a chart of differences between this and their own experiences.

The Watson family in 1905

Text © 2007, Scholastic Ltd. Illustration © Jane Bottomley

2: 3: T14: to pose questions and record these in writing, prior to reading non-fiction to find answers

2: 3: T20: to write non-fiction texts, using texts read as models for own writing

2: 3: W9: to learn new words from reading linked to particular topics

2: 3: T13: to understand the distinction between fact and fiction

2: 3: T19: to make simple notes from non-fiction texts to use in subsequent writing

2: 3: T21: to write non-chronological reports based on structure of known texts

early 20th century, just after the Victorian era

similar to armbands

ordinary, wet-weather umbrellas

quite an event in 1900

Victorians were pioneers in train travel

picture tells us more than text does

description of picture; present tense gives sense of 'reality' and activity

general historical information, past tense

topic words

The Watson family are at the seaside. They have gone there for the day.

Phyllis is six. She is learning to swim using water wings. Her eight-year-old brother Arthur is building a sandcastle. Their mother (Mary) is sitting in the shade. Charles, their father, is reading.

People didn't need to worry about sunburn because they wore their ordinary clothes. If they needed more shade, they used an umbrella.

Many people went to the beach for days out in summer. They went in the morning and came back in the evening. They travelled by train to get there.

The seaside by Patience Coster

Background

This text can be used alongside the previous two to tie in with topic work on the seaside. This is specifically a geographical text, whereas the earlier two explored historical aspects. The extract begins by asking readers to bring their own experiences to the topic. Facts about the seaside are presented under subheadings, and pictures help to explain aspects of the written text. The information is presented using simple language, while introducing a wide range of topic-specific vocabulary. Children can draw on their own experience to pose questions and find answers, writing notes and using these to write non-chronological reports.

What's on the CD-ROM

A purely visual text is provided to encourage less able readers to explore the topic without the reading demands. The pictures can be used in guided reading as discussion starting points and children can make notes about their observations which can be turned into reports.

Discussing the text

● Read the title and introductory questions, keep the rest of the text covered at this point. Ask the children to respond to the questions, noting the effect this has of immediately engaging them by making the text personal. Ask the children to share their knowledge of the topic (drawing on the previous extracts if relevant) and to suggest things they would still like to know and to write these as questions.

● Reveal the rest of the text. Read the subheadings and look at the pictures. Do the children think their questions will be answered in this text? If not, why not? Some children might have surmised that the text would be about what you do at the seaside and will now note that it is actually about geographical features.

● Read the text in conjunction with the pictures, and highlight topic-specific vocabulary as you read. Ask the children to summarise key points from each section. Share children's experiences of the types of beach and features described as you explore the contrasts drawn particularly between rocky and sandy beaches.

● Notice how the text continues to involve the reader by using questions as subheadings and for the first sentence of *What are tides?*

● Focus on the section about tides. Highlight the contrasts and opposites – *rise/fall, high/low*. Point out how the author uses sentences in pairs to emphasise these contrasts.

● Ask the children if their original questions were answered. Record answers where relevant and for others, consider where the information might be found.

Talk, read and write

● Give the children copies of the text (or sections) and ask them to highlight words that relate specifically to the seaside. (These can be used later for spelling and handwriting practice.) Then ask the children to make illustrated glossaries of the seaside words, using dictionaries or encyclopedias if appropriate.

● Ask the children to draw a seaside picture, incorporating as many of the features identified as possible. These could be done as pairs of pictures: *rocky/sandy beach* and *high/low tide*, for example. Ask the children to label the pictures or present them as a 'picture dictionary' for younger readers – with small, labelled pictures of individual features around the main picture.

● In shared or guided writing, model how to use the vocabulary in sentences that describe their pictures. The sentences could be organised under question-headings, such as *What kinds of beaches are there? What do you find on rocky beaches? What happens at high tide?*

● Ask the children to complete their reports independently where possible. Some might need support in guided writing or from a writing frame. Encourage children to add further information, from their own experience or from research in books or on the internet.

Extension

Ask children to suggest other questions about the seaside and to list them as if for a contents page in a non-fiction book. Some children might be able to group and order these by sub-topic. Children could then evaluate each other's contents against their own questions to decide whether the 'book' would answer them. They could also list vocabulary they have learned and organise it alphabetically as for an index.

2: 3: T19: to make simple notes from non-fiction texts to use in subsequent writing

2: 3: T21: to write non-chronological reports based on structure of known text

contrasting types

subheading question works like the 'voice' of the reader

another intriguing question

two-part sentence emphasises contrast

opposites

personalises text – encourages reader to visualise

2: 3: W9: to learn new words from reading linked to particular topics

The Seaside

Have you ever visited the seaside? What did you do there? Did you build sandcastles, explore rock pools, go for a swim?

The seaside is where the land meets the sea. It is a special place, with breaking waves, caves and sand dunes, seaweed, shellfish and sea birds.

Another name for the seaside is the coast. There are different kinds of coast all over the world. Some are rocky with few trees. Other coasts have long sandy beaches and palm trees.

What are Tides?

Did you know that the level of the sea rises and falls? This happens about twice every day. When the level of the sea rises it is called high tide, when it falls this is low tide.

At high tide the beach is mostly covered by the sea. A low tide the sea is sometimes far away and there is a large area of wet sand to play on.

As the tide goes out, seaweed, driftwood and other debris are often left in a line on the beach. This line is the high tide mark.

What Lives on the Seashore?

Different areas of the shore have different types of wildlife. Sea birds gather on the wide, sandy beaches. Rocky parts of the shore may have lots of pools that are home to many animals.

Text extract from "Step by Step Geography: Seas and coasts" by Patience Coster © 1997 Patience Coster (1992, Franklin Watts); photos: background: seas and coast © Craig Jewell; seagull © Kevin Walsh, rocky coast © Andrzej Kobiendzinski

series of questions to engage reader

sentence goes on to list things only found here

less familiar topic words

sentences with same structure detail contrast between tides

it marks (shows) how high tide came

2: 3: T14: to pose questions and record these in writing, prior to reading non-fiction to find answers

2: 3: T20: to write non-fiction texts, using texts read as models for own writing

Contents pages

by Scholastic Ltd

Background

These extracts are from the contents pages of three non-fiction books about the internet. The first is a book specifically about the use of email, the second contains information about a wide range of internet-related topics, the third is about using the internet safely. The extracts encouraging revision of the use of contents pages to access specific information. Using questions as a starting point will also allow children to compare the contents of books on similar topics, to establish which would be most likely to contain particular information and, therefore, answer their questions. The text can be used in conjunction with the following one on email addresses.

What's on the CD-ROM

This text contains just two contents pages: a simplified version of the first core extract and the complete third extract. These will give opportunities for less able readers to explore the use of contents pages and to evaluate the usefulness of particular texts.

Discussing the text

● Before looking at the text, encourage the children to talk about their experience and understanding of the internet and email. Ask them to discuss in pairs what else they would like to know. Share ideas and write some as questions on the board.

● Read the first extract and ask the children what they think it is, where it might be found and what it is used for. Use examples in classroom books to illustrate the location of a contents page at the beginning of a book.

● Ask the children what they think this book might be about. (Using email.) Check understanding of terminology, reminding the children that dictionaries or glossaries in other books on similar topics might provide definitions.

● Ask the children where in the book they would find information about, for example, *Email addresses*. (Pages 10 and 11.) Use other books to show how a page number in the contents list relates to a chapter heading or page title, and is often a double-page spread for ease of reading.

● Read the second extract, and note that this book has just two pages on email, but many other sections on different aspects of the internet.

● Now read the third list. Point out that this book also has information about emails, but has other information about the internet as well. Note that here there is no specific heading for email addresses and it might be on any of pages 36 to 45. Use other books to demonstrate how skim-reading subheadings, for example, might help to narrow the search within a chapter. Ask the children to recall the uses of a glossary and index.

● Compare the layout of each list. Do page numbers or titles come first? Note the alignment of numbers to make for easy reading. Demonstrate on the computer, if appropriate, how to align lists using tab keys.

Talk, read and write

● Choose one question from the board, pick out key words and model how to skim the contents lists to see if it might be answered by any of the books. Let the children repeat this with other questions. Encourage them to be selective about which contents page they search, depending on the question set. Ask the children to evaluate the layouts in terms of ease of searching.

● Provide appropriate books or support the use of simple search engines to enable children to find answers to their questions. If they are using books, help them to select an appropriate one and to skim the contents page (and index if appropriate) to find relevant chapters or sections. Evaluate the accessibility of particular information in different books or on the computer.

● Ask the children to highlight technical vocabulary in the three extracts. Choose one word, discuss its meaning (using reference books if appropriate) and model writing a definition. Organise the children to work in pairs or in a supported group to write definitions for a glossary in the ICT suite.

Extension

Ask children to interview friends and family about their use of the internet and email. Ask them to set out the information as if for a contents page, with page numbers.

2: 3: T15: to use a contents page to find way about text

this page reference begins a range of pages on the same subject

2: 3: T18: to evaluate the usefulness of a text for its purpose

2: 3: W9: to learn new words from reading linked to particular topics

for a book about using the internet safely

Contents

for a book about a wide range of internet topics

Contents

vertical alignment of numbers makes them easy to read

specialist terminology

for a book specifically to do with email

Contents

page number in list relates to page on which chapter heading appears

2: 3: T14: to pose questions and record these in writing, prior to reading non-fiction to find answers

2: 3: T17: to skim-read contents page, to speculate what a text might be about

Email addresses by Mark Wallace and Philippa Wingate

Background

This text explores the constituent parts of an email address, which can be compared to a postal address (perhaps relating to the text on page 70 'Journey of a letter'). The ever-increasing use of electronic, rather than paper-based communication makes this an appropriate topic for young children. The text has a clear structure, moving from the general to the specific, with information presented under subheadings. Technical vocabulary and symbols are usually explained and exemplified within the text.

What's on the CD-ROM

A similar but simpler text is provided on the CD-ROM. It describes the use of electronic mail and email addresses with fewer technical terms. Information is given in short paragraphs with subheadings.

Discussing the text

● Encourage the children to share their knowledge of the topic. Display the school email address (and children's own if known). Some children might be able to explain the different parts of the address (this is what the extract discusses). Ensure that children know how to read aloud an email address (saying *at* for @ and *dot* for .). Ask the children to share ideas for what else they would like to know about email, perhaps drawing on questions in response to the previous text.

● Compare the school's email address with the postal address, and discuss the similar purpose of each: to enable delivery of written communications to the right place and person. Compare the 'concrete' nature of a postal address (it identifies an actual building, in a street/town and so on, and could be found on a map) with the 'abstract' nature of an email address (it is not a place that you could go to). Compare the kinds of communication that are delivered through the postal service to those exchanged via email in school and at home (including 'letters' and photographs).

● Read the introductory paragraph, which gives general information about the topic, and help with any unfamiliar vocabulary. Encourage children to use dictionaries or glossaries as appropriate. Ask pairs to explain to each other what this paragraph

was about and then to highlight key words or phrases on the shared copy.

● Read the first subheading, noting that the question raises what a reader might want to know. Elicit that this section gives more specific information about an individual email address. Highlight the technical terms *user name* and *domain name*, pointing out that these become the next two subheadings. Consider how the labelled example of a typical address clarifies the written text.

● Read the next two sections, highlighting key points. Consider the relevance of each part of the school's email address and children's own if applicable, comparing them with examples in the text. Note that capital letters aren't used (unlike postal addresses): electronic communication is less formal and less governed by 'rules'. Discuss abbreviations, relating to other examples, such as postcodes and text messaging. Stress how important it is to spell the words correctly and put the dots and other symbols in the correct place.

● Explore the information in the *Domain types* box, noting how it is set apart from the main text for impact, with the added clarity of a list format.

Talk, read and write

● In guided groups, highlight technical terminology and write definitions to be added to a glossary of topic-specific vocabulary (perhaps started in work on the previous text).

● Encourage the children to challenge each other to find key words and phrases as quickly as possible. Then, using this and/or other appropriate texts, children can apply scanning techniques to find answers to questions generated earlier. Ask them to make notes then answer in complete sentences.

● Let the children make up email addresses for favourite book characters or celebrities, and write to each other in role.

● Give children the opportunity to exchange genuine emails, perhaps with another school.

Extension

Ask children to find as many email addresses as possible from friends and family. These can be labelled with their constituent parts. How many different domain names can they find?

Text extract and illustrations from "The Usborne Guide to e-mail" by Mark Wallace and Philippa Wingate; illustrated by Christyan Fox © 2000, Usborne Publishing Ltd

2: 3: T19: to make simple notes from non-fiction texts to use in subsequent writing

3: 3: T20: to write non-fiction texts, using texts read as models for own writing

general introduction

specific information about email addresses

subheading raises reader question may want the answer to

technical vocabulary

say 'at'

labelled example clarifies written text

say 'dot'

2: 3: T16: to scan text to find specific examples

2: 3: W9: to learn new words from reading linked to particular topics

Email addresses

All email users have their own, unique email address. This ensures that messages are sent to the correct computers. Your ISP will either give you an address or allow you to choose one.

What does an address look like?

An email address has two main sections: the user name and the domain name. The two sections are separated by an @ symbol, which means "at". Here is a typical address:

mark@usborne.co.uk

user name   "at"   domain name

User name

The user name is often the name or nickname of the person who will receive the email. A name can be used in different ways. If, for example, your name was David Rowe, your user name could be: drowe, davidrowe, davidr, dave or David_Rowe (in the last example, the names are separated by a symbol called an underscore).

People whose email is sent to the same server have email addresses with the same domain name.

Domain name

A domain name is the name of the server to which the message will be sent. For home computer users, this is normally the name of your service provider's computer.

Part of the domain name is called the domain type. This tells you the kind of organisation where the server is located, such as 'gov' for a government organisation, and 'edu' or 'ac' for a school. Some domain types are listed below.

Domain names of computers outside the USA often end in a country code. For example, the code for the United Kingdom is "uk", France is "fr" and Australia is "au".

Dots (.) separate the various parts of the domain name.

Domain types

com or co	a commercial company
edu or ac	an educational establishment
gov	a government organization
net	Internet companies
org	organization

Each person can have an email address with their own user name.

Spiders

by Jason Amber

Background

Many children (and adults!) are afraid of spiders and the facts in this text might put the fear into perspective. Although the text is quite demanding, with technical vocabulary and some complex language structures, the information is presented in an accessible way. The text demonstrates many key features of non-chronological reports, with an introductory paragraph, classification and a description of characteristics (presented as a direct comparison to familiar insects). Literacy work can be linked to science work on animals in the local environment, including treating all living things with respect. Encourage the children *not* to kill spiders.

What's on the CD-ROM

This simplified version presents most of the information visually. The labelled diagram and comparison chart from the core text are retained, but additional text is much reduced. Less able readers can benefit from the information in the main text during shared reading, using the differentiated text in guided and independent tasks to meet similar objectives.

Discussing the text

● Read the title only and share thoughts on the topic, giving the opportunity to discuss feelings about spiders, but also encouraging people to share facts. Write: *What we know about spiders* as a spider(!) diagram or concept map. Now ask the children what else they would like to know about spiders, writing these as questions around the diagram.

● Reveal the rest of the text. Be prepared for reaction to the picture, and explain why it is bigger than life size. Model skim-reading to establish what might be in the text. Talk aloud as you discuss the picture, subheadings, chart and final paragraph, without actually reading the main text. Ask the children what they expect to find in each section and then ask whether they think the text will answer the questions noted on the board.

● Now read the whole text, spending time on any difficult vocabulary and ideas. Model word-level strategies for reading as appropriate, including syllabification and breaking down compounds. List technical vocabulary as you come across it, allowing the children to use dictionaries if appropriate to explore meanings. (Some of the more complex language structures might need elaboration, such as the sentence containing *whereas*.)

● Ask the children to summarise each section of the text, by identifying two or three key points. Note that the labelled diagram and chart are themselves summaries. Does the text contain the information they expected?

● Highlight the commas used in the lists of insects and arachnids, noting how they separate items for clarity. Point out that there is no comma after the final item in the list.

Talk, read and write

● Highlight key words in one of the questions generated earlier that can be answered from the text. Ask the class to skim-read to establish which section might contain the answer and then scan that section for key words. Write the answer in note form and then work together to turn it into a sentence. Now ask the children to use similar strategies to answer other questions. Provide additional reference sources for information not covered by this text.

● In guided reading, practise turning statements from the text into questions. For example, the first clause becomes *How many species of spider are there?* Ask the children to take statements from the text, turn them into questions, then add them back to the text as subheadings, which will help the next reader to find specific facts. This format of question and answer could be used for a presentation to the class or school.

● Children can use the text to draw and label comparative pictures of an insect and a spider. Encourage some children to use other reference sources to supplement the information. Help them to write sentences to act as captions (using the conjunction *whereas,* if appropriate, to emphasise the contrast).

Extension

Ask children to choose two similar, but different, 'types' within a topic with which they are familiar, such as cats and dogs. Ask them to make a chart, using the model from the text, to identify key features and how they differ.

2: 3: T17: to skim-read illustrations, chapter headings and subheadings, to speculate what a text might be about

2: 3: W9: to learn new words from reading linked to particular topics

2: 3: S6: to turn statements into questions

large picture at beginning of text catches eye

chart presents information briefly; comparisons can be seen quickly

Text extract from "Literacy World: Stage 4: Spiders and how they hunt" by Jason Amber © 1999, Reed Educational and Professional Publishing Ltd (1999, Heinemann Educational Publishers); photos: web © Valentina Frate, spider © Maarten Uilenbroek

Spiders

Introduction

There are over 30,000 different species of spider, and they can be found all over the world. They are able to survive in hot and cold climates in deserts, rainforests and grasslands. One can even live underwater. The only areas in which spiders are not found are the Arctic, the Antarctic and in deep oceans. All spiders are carnivores, but different species have different methods of catching their prey.

Arachnids

It is often thought that spiders are insects, but they are in fact a different kind of animal called an arachnid. There are significant differences between the two. Insects have six legs, whereas arachnids have eight legs. Typical insects are ants, bees, beetles and butterflies. Typical arachnids include spiders, scorpions and ticks.

All spiders:

have eight legs; have large jaws and sharp fangs to bite prey; have spinnerets that can spin silk for making webs.

Most spiders:

have eight eyes, but many cannot see very well; have hairs on their legs that can sense the movement of other animals nearby; have fangs through which they can inject poison into their prey;

Some spiders:

have six, four or two eyes; have no eyes at all – these are cave-dwelling spiders.

Labels on spider diagram: claw, fangs, jaw, head and thorax, leg, abdomen, spinnerets, hairs, eyes

	Insects	Arachnids
Legs	6	8
Antennae	2	none
Wings	most have 2 or 4	none
Has a poisonous bite or sting	some	nearly all
Eats plants	some	none
Eats other animals	some	all

lots of topic vocabulary

animal caught for food

species classification (like birds, insects, mammals)

connective indicating contrast/opposite

commas separate items in lists

2: 3: T14: to pose questions and record these in writing, prior to reading non-fiction to find answers

2: 3: T20: to write non-fiction texts, using texts read as models for own writing

2: 3: S4: to use commas in lists

Healthy food

by Jillian Powell

Background

This non-fiction text on healthy eating makes use of text, pictures and labelled diagrams. It demonstrates key features of non-chronological reports, such as a general introduction followed by more specific detail, using the present tense. It introduces technical vocabulary (such as *nutrients* and names for some of the main food groups), and the illustrations aid understanding. Healthy eating is a topical issue for schools and children and has direct relevance to their lives. Literacy work can be linked to health and growth in science.

What's on the CD-ROM

This text contains similar information, but in a simpler way. It presents key information about healthy and unhealthy food in simple language that addresses the reader directly. It avoids technical vocabulary, allowing less able readers to access the information more readily. Shared reading of the core text can introduce less able readers to the technical vocabulary, but this simpler text will allow exploration of non-chronological reports in guided and independent tasks.

Discussing the text

● Before reading, ask the children to look over the text and consider whether it is fiction or non-fiction. Is it a story or does it give facts and information? How do they know? The children should be able to state that the layout identifies it as non-fiction.

● Now read the title and ask the children what information they expect to find in the text. What do they already know about healthy food? Take some time to discuss what foods they eat that are healthy and unhealthy.

● Read the first two paragraphs. Notice that the first sentence introduces the topic and the rest then gives more detail about healthy food. Explain difficult vocabulary as it arises, noting that non-fiction texts often have unfamiliar words because they introduce technical terms specific to the topic. Model word-level strategies for reading difficult words, such as syllabification, prefixes and suffixes and compound words.

● Draw attention to the use of commas to separate the items in the lists of foods. Write the items as a column list. Cover the original sentence. Ask the children to help you reform the sentence. Where do the commas go?

● Ask pairs to discuss the key points from this part of the text. What did they learn? Relate this to their experience and what they think about the foods mentioned as healthy and unhealthy. Ask children to highlight important words and phrases on the text.

● Look at the picture of the ice cream and read the text below it. Recap that this is called a caption and tells us about the picture.

● Read the information in the box, encouraging children to point to the food items as they are mentioned. Note that the sentence in the corner gives a summary of what makes a healthy diet. Allow children to give their personal responses to the meal items shown in the picture.

● Identify and highlight presentational features of the text – title, subheading, pictures, caption, diagram – and discuss the purpose and effect of each.

Talk, read and write

● Ask the children to make a list of foods mentioned in the text under two headings – *healthy* and *unhealthy foods*. They can then add (using pictures or words as appropriate) their own items, drawing on their personal knowledge and experience or through research of other texts or the internet. These could be made into posters for the classroom.

● Give the children copies of the text with key words omitted and a word bank to select the correct word from, such as *(un)healthy, nutrient, wholegrain, treats*.

● In a guided session, help children to make a glossary of food-related terms, using dictionaries, encyclopedias or other sources.

● Practise the use of commas for lists, by providing sentence starters for children to complete.

Extension

Ask children to draw and label what they eat during one day, at school and at home. Then they should list the healthy foods and unhealthy foods in sentences. They could also find pictures in magazines or on food labels to illustrate their sentences for display.

2: 3: T13: to understand the distinction between fact and fiction

2: 3: W9: to learn new words from reading linked to particular topics

present tense verbs

use syllabification to read

commas separate items in a list

photos show examples of food from each of the groups

title reflects content of text

general introductory sentence – later sentences give more detail

prefix 'un'; suffix 'y'

caption

2: 3: S4: to use commas in lists

2: 3: W2: to reinforce work on discriminating syllables in reading and spelling from previous term

Healthy food

Having a healthy, balanced diet means eating lots of different foods which give your body the nutrients it needs. Healthy foods include natural foods like wholemeal bread and wholegrain rice, beans and lentils. They contain lots of important nutrients like carbohydrates and vitamins but no added sugar, salt or additives. Organic food is food farmed without using chemicals.

Unhealthy foods are foods like sweets, lollies, cakes, biscuits and fizzy drinks. They contain lots of sugar, fat and additives and no important nutrients.
It is best to eat them as treats now and again.

▲ Ice creams are eaten as treats now and again.

A balanced diet
There are five main food groups.

Fatty and sugary foods like cakes and biscuits

Meat, poultry and fish

Fruit and vegetables

Starchy foods like cereals, potatoes, pasta, rice

Dairy foods like milk, butter, cheese

MILK

A balanced meal contains foods from each of the first four groups. Group five foods should only be eaten as treats now and again.

Text extract from "Food and your health" by Jillian Powell © 1997, Hodder Wayland; photos © 2006, Jupiter Images Corporation

Rainforests

by Michael Chinery

Background

This text considers an important global ecological issue of the 21st century. Although the topic will be beyond the immediate experience of the children, they might be aware of some of the issues from television, magazines or adult conversation. It seems never too early to raise children's awareness of the wider world. The text might provide links to the geography curriculum and to aspects of citizenship. It could also be linked to the earlier extract on elephants (page 82) in terms of conservation issues. Although this is a challenging topic, technical vocabulary is often explained within the text and these explanations are simple. The text contains subheadings, allowing children to develop appropriate reading skills to access information.

What's on the CD-ROM

A simpler version of similar information, under the same subheadings, is provided here. Much of the key vocabulary is retained, but the sentence structure is generally less complex, enabling less able readers to engage with the issues. This text can be used in guided work to develop strategies such as skimming and scanning with less demanding text.

Discussing the text

● Read the title and subheadings, and explore the pictures. Ask the children what the text is about, whether it is fiction or non-fiction and how they know. Encourage everyone to share in pairs, and then with the class, their prior knowledge of the topic.

● Now ask the children to suggest things they would like to know about rainforests. Write some of these on the board as questions. Read the headings again, to see that most of these are expressed as questions.

● Read the text with children. Ask them to discuss it in pairs and then feed back one thing they have learned. Ask the children to identify their points in the text and highlight key words or phrases.

● Re-read the text, speculating about meanings of unfamiliar vocabulary and using dictionaries as appropriate to establish definitions.

● Pinpoint rainforest locations on a globe or in an atlas. Ask the children what they think it would be like to live in a place where it is hot and wet all the time. Note that plants grow well in these conditions.

● Use a familiar example to illustrate the surprising fact revealed in *Do you know?*, for example, a pizza cut into 20 pieces, where more than half the topping is on just one portion!

● Note that the first two sections of the text give information about rainforests, while the second two *explain* the problems associated with them. You might relate this to work on explanatory texts from Term 2, recalling that these explain why or how something happens.

● If appropriate, consider alternative viewpoints on the issues, such as that of farmers who need land to grow crops. Talk about the distinction between *fact* and *opinion*. Explain that this paragraph contains facts, but is presented from a particular point of view.

Talk, read and write

● In guided groups, using questions generated earlier (and those from the text subheadings), model how to use pictures, captions, subheadings and highlighted key words to find answers. Could all the questions posed be answered from this text? If not, how might the children find answers? Ask: *How could you tell whether a non-fiction book would answer your questions?* Revise how a contents list, index and headings can all be used to find out what information a particular text contains.

● Ask the children to draw or paint 'before and after' pictures to illustrate the effect of felling rainforests, drawing on the information and illustrations in the text and other sources if appropriate. Encourage them to label and/or caption their pictures, using key words and phrases identified earlier.

● Some children could draw and label a diagram of the greenhouse effect.

Extension

Ask children to choose a familiar topic. They can then write several statements about that topic, some of which are facts and some of which are opinions. Other children can decide whether each statement is fact or opinion.

2: 3: T20: to write non-fiction texts, using texts read as models for own writing

2: 3: T17: to skim-read illustrations, chapter headings and subheadings to speculate what a book might be about

explanation of the greenhouse effect and the link with rainforests

problems associated with rainforests

technical vocabulary

general information about rainforests

WHERE DO RAINFORESTS GROW?

Rainforests grow in places where there is lots of rain. Most rainforests are found in the tropics, on either side of the equator. Most of the plants there are evergreen – they never drop all their leaves at once, but grow the whole year round in the hot, steamy atmosphere. Animals live at all levels in the forest, from the ground to the tree-tops.

Do you know?
Some rainforests are huge, but altogether they still only cover about one-twentieth of the Earth's surface. Even so, scientists believe that the rainforests contain more than half of the world's plant and animal species.

WHY ARE RAINFORESTS IN DANGER?

Rainforests are among the most threatened places on Earth. Millions of trees are cut down each year for timber. Huge areas are also felled every day to make way for farming. Thousands of animals are probably becoming extinct every year because there is nowhere left for them to live. Even if new trees are planted, these places will never get their original wildlife back again.

Many kinds of beautiful forest birds and insects will never be seen again because their forest homes are being cut down. The problem is especially bad in South America and South-East Asia.

Greenhouse effect
Every time we breathe, we give out a gas called carbon dioxide. The same gas is made in car engines and whenever we burn anything. It forms a layer round the Earth and traps heat, just like greenhouse glass. The heat warms the Earth and can cause droughts and other big changes in the world's weather. Trees use up carbon dioxide, so cutting down the rain forests is making this 'Greenhouse Effect' even worse.

Text extracts and illustrations from Questions and Answers - Rainforest Animals by Michael Chinery, illustrated by David Holmes and Bernard Robinson © 1995, Kingfisher Publications plc.

subheadings expressed as questions - suggests there are things the reader may want to find out

2: 3: T16: to scan a text to find specific sections

How we made a puppet whale

First, we got some card, a pencil, a pair of scissors, a paper fastener, some sticky tape and two sticks.

Then, we drew the body and tail of a whale on the card.

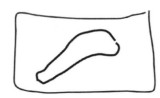

Next, we drew its mouth on another part of the card.

After that, we cut out the two parts.

To make the mouth move, we joined the body and the mouth with a paper fastener.

Finally, we stuck one stick on the body and one stick on the mouth with sticky tape.

When you move the sticks, the whale's mouth opens and shuts.

Text © 2007, Sue Taylor; notebook clip art © Nova Developments

50 Shared texts **Non-fiction ● Year 2**

Puppets

Some puppets are 3D images of people or animals which are moved by hand. They can be used to tell stories. They can be held and moved with sticks. Some puppets can make shadows on a screen.

How you can do it

You will need:
pencil, card, scissors, paper fastener, sticky tape, two long sticks.

1 Draw a simple animal shape.

2 Choose which piece of the animal you want to move. This could be the head or tail.

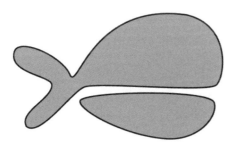

3 Draw the two parts separately on a piece of card.

4 Cut them out and use a paper fastener to join the two parts together.

5 Tape a stick to the back of each part.

Text extract and images from "Arts and Crafts Around the World" © 1997, Reed Educational and Professional Publishing Ltd courtesy of Harcourt Education; puppet photo © 2006, Jupiter Images Corporation

Easy pop-ups

Hippo ballerina
This hippopotamus ballet dancer has a pop-up ballet skirt.

You will need:
a piece of pink paper 20 × 10cm (8 × 4in); a piece of thick, white paper 19 × 19cm (7½ × 7½in); a pencil; felt-tip pens; glue.

Text extract and illustration from "The Usborne Book of Pop-ups" by Richard Dungworth and Ray Gibson; Illustration by Teri Gower © 1995, Usborne Publishing Ltd

1. Lay the pink paper down with its long edges at the sides. Fold down a 2cm (¾in) strip at the top edge.

2. Turn the paper over and fold down another 2cm (¾in). Repeat this step until you run out of paper.

3. Put glue on one side of the strip. Fold it in half so that its ends meet. Press while the glue dries.

4. Fold the piece of white paper in half to make a card. Draw a hippo ballerina across the inside of the fold.

5. Glue the accordion strip onto your ballerina, so that its folded end is against the middle crease.

6. Put some glue on top of the strip and carefully close the card. Press down while the glue dries.

7. When you open the card, the pink accordion-folded strip will fan out like a ballet skirt.

16

Swedish hanging biscuits

You will need:
225g (8oz) plain flour
½ teaspoon
   bicarbonate of soda
icing sugar
pinch of ground
   cloves
¾ teaspoon ground
   ginger
¾ teaspoon
   cinnamon
115g (4oz) margarine
115g (4oz) dark
   brown sugar
1 egg white

2 large bowls
Christmas biscuit
   cutters
sieve
baking tray
clingfilm
rolling pin
fish slice
wooden spoon
fat straw
fine ribbon
cooling
   rack

Set oven to:
180ºC, 350ºF Gas Mark 4

Hint
Don't put the hole too near the top of the biscuit or it will break when you hang it up.

Cream the margarine and sugar well, then beat in the egg white.

Sift the dry ingredients together in another bowl.

Add a little at a time to the creamed mixture and blend together well to make a dough.

Wrap the dough in clingfilm and chill it for 30 minutes in the refrigerator, or ten minutes in the freezer.

Roll the dough out on a clean, floured surface, until it is about 5mm (¼in) thick.

Press biscuit cutters firmly into the dough. Peel away the extra dough.

Lift the shapes onto an ungreased baking tray, using a fish slice.

Press the end of a straw into the top of each shape, to make a hole.

Bake in the oven for ten to twelve minutes. Take out and cool on a cooling rack.

Text extract and illustrations from "You and Your Child: Christmas" by Ray Gibson © 1991, Usborne Publishing Ltd

How to make wholemeal bread rolls

Makes 12 rolls
Preparation time:
1½ hours
Cooking time:
40 minutes

Ingredients:
25g dried yeast
1 teaspoon sugar
225ml warm water
375g wholemeal flour
1 tablespoon sunflower oil

Equipment:
Large bowl
Measuring jug
Teaspoon
Tablespoon
Clingfilm
Baking tray

THE OVEN, THE BAKING TRAY AND THE ROLLS WILL BE VERY HOT. DO NOT TOUCH! ASK AN ADULT!

Method:

1   Wash your hands.

2   Put the warm water in a jug and stir in the sugar. Stir until the sugar dissolves. Add the yeast and mix well.

3   Leave the mixture in a warm place for about ten minutes. Watch the yeast start to bubble and froth!

4   Put the flour into a large bowl. Stir in the salt and sunflower oil.

5   Pour in the yeast and water mixture and stir with a wooden spoon.

6   When the mixture sticks together in a ball, put it onto the table. Knead it well with your hands for about ten minutes to make the dough smooth and springy. You might need some extra flour so the dough doesn't stick to the table.

7   Put the dough in a clean bowl. Cover it with clingfilm and leave it in a warm place for about 1 hour to rise. Watch it grow!

8   When the dough has doubled in size, take it out of the bowl and knead it again for five minutes.

9   Cut it into 12 pieces and shape each piece into a ball. Put the balls on a baking tray. Cover them and leave them to rise again for about 20 minutes.

10   Meanwhile, turn on the oven to 200ºC/400ºF/ Gas mark 6.

11   When the rolls have doubled in size, bake them for about 20 minutes until they are golden brown.

12   Put the rolls on a wire rack to cool.

Text © 2007, Sue Taylor; photo © 2006, Jupiter Images Corporation

Term 1: Instructional texts

Route map

This is a map of the way to Lucy and John's school. It shows all the things that they pass on the way. This is called a route map.

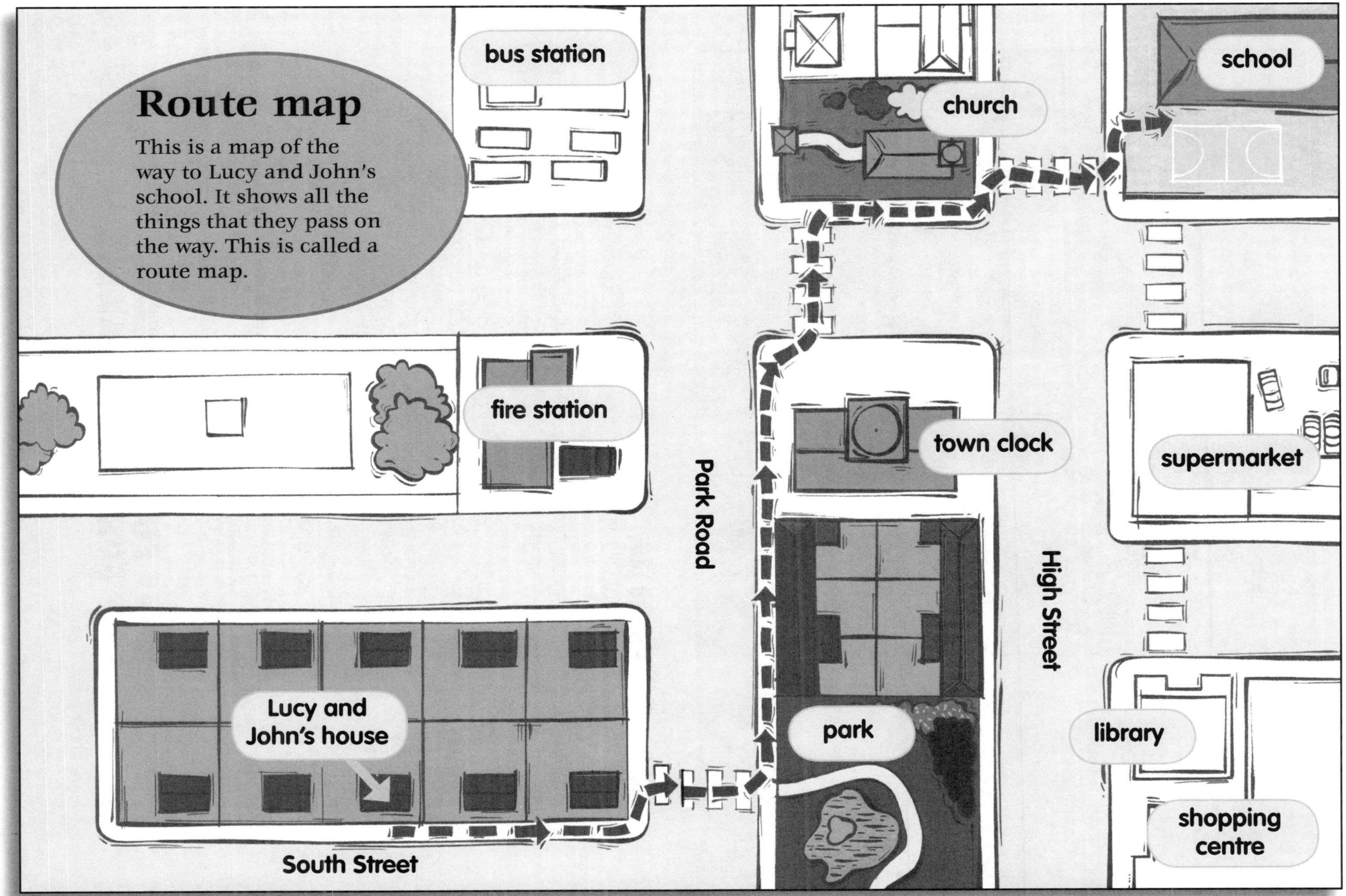

N

school

supermarket

shopping centre

library

church

town clock

park

High Street

Park Road

bus station

fire station

Lucy and John's house

South Street

Text and Illustrations "Discovery World Stage F: Maps" © 1997, Reed Educational and Professional Publishing Ltd; illustrations Roger Fereday/Linda Rogers Associates

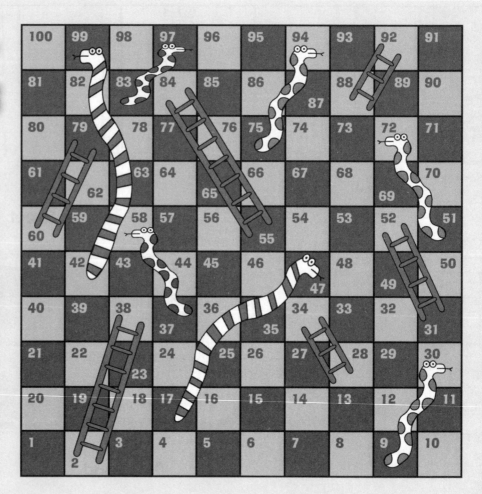

SNAKES AND LADDERS

How to play Snakes and Ladders

This is a game for 2–4 players. Keeps you busy at wet playtime!

This is what you need
- one Snakes and Ladders board
- one dice
- a counter for each player

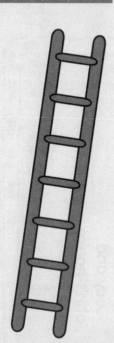

How to play

First, put all the counters on the first square (number 1).

Then, throw the dice to decide who will go first. The highest number starts.

Now, take it in turns to throw the dice and move your counter the number of spaces that the dice shows.

😊 If you land on the bottom of a ladder, go straight up it to the top.

☹ If you land on the head of a snake, go right down to its tail.

The winner is the first person to get to the last square (number 100).

HAVE FUN AND WATCH OUT FOR THOSE SNAKES!

Text © 2007, Sue Taylor

How to play hopscotch

**Lots of fun in the playground! Play by yourself
or with your friends.**

What you need:

- a playground
- a piece of chalk
- a beanbag for each player

1. First draw the hopscotch grid on the playground with chalk.

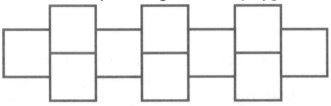

2. Next put the numbers from 1 to 10 in the squares.

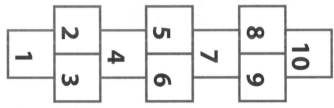

3. Now hop and jump in the squares. Start at number 1 (one) and finish at number 10 (ten).

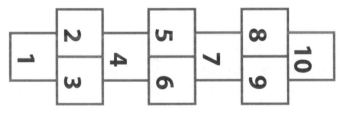

start ⟶ finish

4. Then turn round and hop and jump back again.

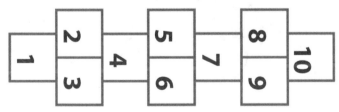

finish ⟵ start

5. When you are good at this, throw a beanbag into a square. Hop and jump from 1 (one) to 10 (ten) and back again, missing out the square with the beanbag in. Try to pick up the beanbag on the way back.

6. If you enjoy this game, make a bigger hopscotch with all the numbers up to 20 (twenty). This will keep you very fit!

Text © 2007, Sue Taylor; photo © 2006, Jupiter Images Corporation

String games
Cup and Saucer

You will need a piece of string about 1½ metres long, with the ends tied together to make a loop.

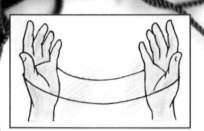

1 Loop the string across both of your palms and behind your little fingers and thumbs.

2 Now reach across with the first finger of your right hand and pick up the string that runs across the left palm. Pull your hands apart.

3 Now reach across with the first finger of your left hand and pick up the string that runs across the right palm.

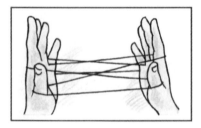

4 Pull your hands apart again.

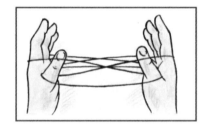

5 Next reach over with both thumbs and hook them under the string on the far side of each first finger.

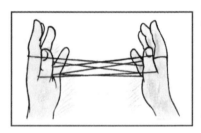

6 Pull your thumbs back to where they started from. You will have two loops on each thumb.

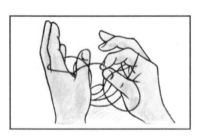

7 Using your mouth or your other hand if you can, pull the bottom loops off your thumbs. These loops will have to pass over the top ones to come off.

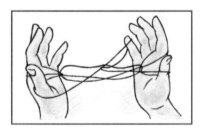

8 Now drop the loops from both little fingers and pull your hands apart.

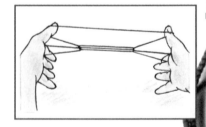

9 Tilt your thumbs up so the **Cup and Saucer** are right-side up.

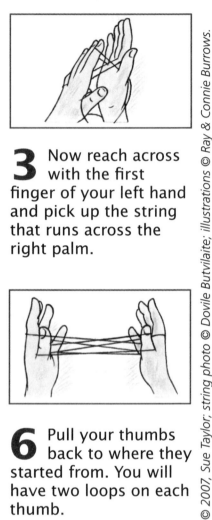

Text © 2007, Sue Taylor; string photo © Dovile Butvilaite; illustrations © Ray & Connie Burrows.

MIXING COLOURS TO PAINT A RAINBOW

WHAT YOU NEED:
Red, yellow and blue paint
6 clean pots to put paint in
A thick paintbrush
A pot of clean water
A big piece of paper to paint a rainbow

Yellow, red and blue are called the **primary colours**. When you mix two primary colours, you get the secondary colours.

First put some **yellow**, **red** and **blue** paint in three separate pots. Don't forget to wash your brush before you put it into a different colour.

To make **orange** paint, take some of the yellow paint and put it in another pot. Wash your brush in clean water. Now add some red paint to this new pot of yellow and mix well. What colour do you get?

To make **green** paint, take some more of the yellow paint and put it in another clean pot. (Remember to wash your brush every time you use a new colour.)
Add some blue paint and mix well. What colour is it?

To make **purple** paint, put some blue paint in the last clean pot. (Wash your brush!) Add some red paint and mix. What colour do you see?

You now have six colours – **red**, **yellow**, **orange**, **green**, **blue** and **purple**. These are the colours of the rainbow.
Paint a big rainbow, like the one in the picture at the top.

Text © 2007, Sue Taylor

Painting butterflies

You will need:

A piece of plain A4 paper
Thick paintbrushes – one for each colour of paint that you use
Paint (thick paint made from powder is best, or poster paint from a bottle. You will need about 4 bright colours)
A pot of clean water
An apron

1. First you need to fold the paper in half and then open it out again.

2. Next you put blobs of different coloured paint on one side of the paper.

3. Then you need to fold the paper in half again, with the paint inside. You can press the paper together and rub your hand across the paper to spread the paint inside.

4. Now you can open up the paper again and look at your butterfly.

You could add a body and antennae. If you cut out your butterfly you can hang it up in the classroom.

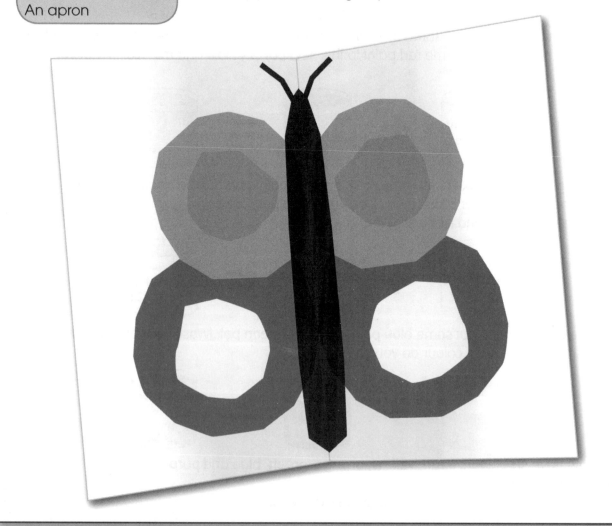

Text © 2007, Sue Taylor

How to look after a hamster

Before buying a hamster, ask for advice from a pet shop or a vet and buy a book about hamsters. Hamsters can be fun but they need to be cared for.

You will need:

• A hamster cage – it must be spacious, have a nestbox and be escape-proof.
• A food container – it must be quite heavy so that it can't be tipped over easily.
• A water container – upside-down bottles are best.
• Exercise ladders or wheels – so your hamster doesn't get too fat or lazy!
• Bedding – straw or hay sold in your pet shop is best.
• Floor covering – you can buy sawdust or woodshavings from the pet shop.
• Food – seeds and nuts, fruit and vegetables.

What you need to do:

• Put the cage somewhere not too hot and not too cold.
• Clean out the cage at least once a week.
• Feed your hamster once a day.
• Wash the food bowl every day.
• Give your hamster fresh water every day.
• Always handle your hamster gently and carefully.

Look after your hamster well and you will have lots of fun together!

Text © 2007, Sue Taylor; photos © Photodisc Inc

Making sentences with Roamer

Turn on your Roamer.

Press to go forwards.

Press to go backwards.

Then press a number (n) to tell Roamer how far to go.

Press (w) to tell Roamer to wait.

Press a number (n) to tell Roamer how long to wait.

Now you can make sentences.

Always press   before you start.

can

make

you

me

Roamer

makes

laugh

 Valiant Technology Ltd, 3 Grange Mills, Weir Road, London SW12 0NE, Tel: 020-8673 2233 • Fax: 020-8673 6333, • e-mail: info@valiant-technology.com • Web site: www.valiant-technology.com

Text extract and illustrations from Valiant Technology's "The Roamer Literacy Pack" © 2005, Valiant Technology

Classroom rules

You should always be polite and kind to everyone.

You should listen to other people when they have something to say.

You must put your hand up if you have something to say.

You should keep the classroom tidy.

You must always use equipment carefully.

You should work quietly and sensibly.

Text © 2007, Sue Taylor; pinboard photo © Davide Guglielmo

How to 'grow' a Japanese Wishing Tree

Make your wishes and hang them on the tree!
Japanese people hang their wishes on a special tree.
They believe that their wishes will come true when
their leaves blow away.
Yours will stay on the tree for everyone to read.

First you will need to ask your teacher to help you draw the trunk and branches of a tree on a big display board.

I wish...

Then draw your leaf on light green paper and cut it out very carefully. You can use the template on the right.

Now write **five wishes** on your leaf, one from each little leaf:

one wish for yourself

one wish for your friends

one wish for your family

one wish for your school

one wish for the whole world

Finally, hang your leaf on the tree. Use Blu-Tack or drawing pins.

Think carefully about your wishes before you write.

Text © 2007, Sue Taylor

Be safe with fireworks!

Spot the danger!

Follow the rules

💥 Keep all your pets indoors.

💥 Store your fireworks in a closed tin.

💥 Never play with fireworks.

💥 Don't put fireworks in your pockets.

💥 Always let an adult light fireworks.

💥 Stand well back when a firework has been lit.

💥 Wear gloves to hold sparklers.

illustration © Ray & Corinne Burrows/Beehive Illustration

Making dummy fireworks 1

Age range
Seven to nine

Group size
Individuals

What you need
Copies of nets for pyramids (see page 120), cardboard tubes, felt-tipped pens, scissors, adhesive.

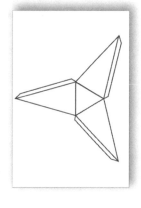

What to do
First discuss the names of the various 3D shapes with the children. They can then make dummy fireworks using the copies of the nets and the cardboard cylinders. Cut out the nets and then decorate them with felt-tipped pens (this should be done before the shapes are stuck). Make sure the children make their design so that any writing will be the right way up when the shape is stuck together. Ask the children to make up exotic names for their fireworks.

The finished shapes can be displayed against a 'fire' painting and the firework code cartoons. Alternatively a background of acrostic words built up on the word 'fireworks' could be used as a background. These words could illustrate the sights, sounds and atmosphere of a firework display.

Text extract from
"Bright Ideas: Festivals" by Jill Bennett and Archie Millar © 1988, Jill Bennett and Archie Millar (1988 Scholastic Ltd):

whale

whale whales

NOUN A **whale** is a huge mammal that lives in the sea. Whales breathe through an opening in the top of their head.

what

ADJECTIVE or PRONOUN **1 What** is used in questions. *What time is it? What is your name?*

PRONOUN **2** You can use **what** to refer to information abut something. *I don't know* **what** *you mean.*

What about PHRASE You say **what about** at the beginning of a question when you are making a suggestion or offer. *What about a sandwich?*

wheat

NOUN **Wheat** is a cereal plant grown for its grain, which is used to make flour.

wheel wheels

NOUN A **wheel** is a circular object which turns round on a rod fixed to its centre. Wheels are fitted under things such as cars, bicycles and prams so that they can move along.

wheelbarrow wheelbarrows

NOUN A **wheelbarrow** is a small cart with a single wheel at the front.

wheelchair wheelchairs

NOUN A **wheelchair** is a chair with large wheels for use by people who find walking difficult or impossible.

when

ADVERB **1** You use **when** to ask what time something happened or will happen. *When are you leaving?*

CONJUNCTION **2** You use **when** to refer to a certain time. *I met him* **when** *we were at school together.*

where

ADVERB **1** You use **where** to ask questions about place. *Where is my book?*

CONJUNCTION **2** You use **where** to talk about the place in which something is situated or happening. *I don't know* **where** *we are.*

whether

CONJUNCTION You can use **whether** instead of **if**. *I don't know* **whether** *I can go.*

which

ADJECTIVE **1** You use **which** to ask for information about something when there are two or more possibilities. *Which room are you in?*

PRONOUN **2** You also use **which** when you are going to say more about something you have already mentioned. *We have a car* **which** *is dropping to bits.*

a b c d e f g h i j k l m n o p q r s t u v **Ww** x y z

Text extract from "Collins Junior Dictionary" compiled by Evelyn Goldsmith © 2000, HarperCollins Publishers Ltd (2000, Collins); photos: whale © Keran McKenzie, wheat © Frank Van Den Berg, wheel © Helmut Gevert, wheelbarrow © Davide Guglielmo

ba-bl

- **baby**
  a newly born or very young animal

- **battery**
  a small container that makes and stores electricity
  ▲ **See also:** electricity

- **bean**
  a large seed that grows inside the long pod of a plant
  ▲ **See also:** pod, seed

- **blind**
  unable to see

- **blossom**
  small flowers on trees in spring
  ▲ **See also:** flower

ad-ar

- **adult**
  a fully grown animal or plant

- **amphibian**
  an animal that lives some of its time on land but lays its eggs in water

- **animal**
  a living thing that breathes and moves about

- **arm**
  the part of a person's body between the shoulder and the hand
  ▲ **See also:** hand

Text extract from "Science Dictionary" © 1997, Reed Educational; photos: frog © Luc Sesselle, ballet dancers arm © Laura Kennedy, baby © Christian Carollo, beans © Keith Syviaski, blossom © Chris Chidsey

50 Shared texts Non-fiction ● Year 2

-teen

-teen A suffix that means a number from 13 to 19.

ten A whole number made up of ten <u>ones</u>, or <u>units</u>. It is written as 10. <u>Multiples</u> of <u>ten</u> include numbers ending in 0, such as 20, 30, 40 and 50. Something that is split into ten <u>equal</u> parts is made up of ten tenths.

third This is not a whole number, it is a fraction. A third is one of three <u>equal</u> parts that make up a whole.

thousand A whole number made up of <u>ten</u> <u>hundreds</u>. It is written as 1000. Something that is split into one thousand <u>equal</u> parts is made up of a thousand thousandths.

times Another way of saying <u>multiplied</u> by.

▲ *This flag is divided into different coloured **thirds**.*

times-tables These are lists of whole numbers <u>multiplied</u> by other numbers. For example, the two times table starts as follows:

1 x 2 = 2
2 x 2 = 4
3 x 2 = 6
4 x 2 = 8
5 x 2 = 10
6 x 2 = 12
and so on.

total The result of adding a groups of numbers together – how much they make altogether.

◄ *This girl has **thousands** of hairs on her head.*

Text © 2007, Scholastic Ltd; photos: hair © Darrell Coomes, flag © Vullioud Piere Andre

S s

shore   *rhyming sound -ore*

before	bore	core	chore
explore	more	score	store

-ore rhymes with -oar

boar   oar   roar   soar

-ore also rhymes with -aw

claw	draw	gnaw	jaw	law
paw	raw	saw	straw	thaw

Other words that rhyme with shore

door	floor
for	or	nor
four	pour	your
war	dinosaur

Dinah Shore dreamed she saw a dinosaur
Knock on her window with its claw.
Dinah Shore dreamed she saw a dinosaur
Peeping round her bedroom door.
Dinah Shore dreamed she saw a dinosaur
Fast asleep on the kitchen floor.
Dinah Shore dreamed she saw a dinosaur
Wake up and give a mighty **ROAR!**

Text extract and illustration from "Oxford First Rhyming Dictionary" by John Foster; illustration © 2003, John Foster; text © 2003, Oxford University Press)

50 Shared texts Non-fiction ● Year 2

a b c d e f g h i j k l m n o p q r s t u v w x y z

Thesaurus
Find a better word!

bad

Bad is a very common word and it has a lot of different meanings. You can often use another word instead.

What a bad child!
You could say **naughty** instead.

The king was a bad man.
You could say **wicked** instead.

She is bad at spelling.
You could say **poor** instead.

There's a bad smell coming from the dustbin.
You could say **nasty** or **revolting** or **horrible** instead.

I feel bad about forgetting his birthday.
You could say **awful** or **dreadful** or **terrible** instead.

The opposite of **bad** is **good**.

good

Good is a very common word and it has a lot of different meanings. You can often use another word instead.

This is a good book.
You could say **enjoyable** instead.

Be a good boy.
You could say **well-behaved** instead.

He was a good king.
You could say **kind** or **nice** instead.

There's a good smell coming from the oven.
You could say **nice** or **lovely** or **fine** instead.

This work is good.
You could say **well done** instead.

The opposite of **good** is **bad**.

a b c d e f g h i j k l m n o p q r s t u v w x y z

Text extracts from Oxford First Thesaurus by Andrew Delahunty © 2002, Andrew Delahunty (2002, Oxford University Press); Photos © 2006, Jupiter Images Corporation

CLASS 2 DIRECTORY OF ADDRESSES AND TELEPHONE NUMBERS

ABBOTT, R,	6 West Drive, Hinton, Essex, AT12 3JG	(01231) 345986
ADAMS, J,	17 New Street, Hinton, Essex, AT12 7PL	(01231) 485967
AKHTAR, M,	44 Kent Road, Hinton, Essex, AT12 3KU	(01231) 440958
BRIDGES, D,	25 Bond Street, Hinton, Essex, AT12 9OP	(01231) 439472
CHEUNG, C,	Flat 3, Fern Court, Pine Walk, Hinton, Essex, AT12 8LJ	(01231) 394810
COOK, C,	31 Queens Road, Hinton, Essex, AT12 4MJ	(01231) 728163
COOPER, A,	14 Tower Lane, Hinton, Essex, AT12 5HG	(01231) 473620
CROSS, S,	37 Queens Road, Hinton, Essex, AT12 4MJ	(01231) 384910
ELDERTON, M,	Everglades, 3 Riverside, Hinton, Essex, AT12 1PT	(01231) 759483
FERRARO, L,	12a Sunnyside Drive, Hinton, Essex, AT12 5DG	(01231) 747738
HOLMES, J,	1 Dukes Court, New Street, Hinton, Essex, AT12 7IJ	(01231) 488294
HUSSAIN, D,	99 Kingswood Crescent, Hinton, Essex, AT12 7DR	(01231) 401938
KAVANAGH, R,	15 Long Road, Hinton, Essex, AT12 1OL	(01231) 485994
KHALID, S,	42 Bond Street, Hinton, Essex, AT12 9KR	(01231) 374822
OAKLEY, S,	Flat 18, Fern Court, Pine Walk, Hinton, Essex, AT12 8LJ	(01231) 728362
PIGGOTT, C,	43 Ross Road, Hinton, Essex, AT12 9PD	(01231) 451436
POULTON, A,	34 Cox Court, New Street, Hinton, Essex, AT12 2IL	(01231) 374856
SMITH, M,	34b Park Road, Hinton, Essex, AT12 8AD	(01231) 737265
STEWART, L,	165 High Street, Hinton, Essex, AT12 2AH	(01231) 746302
WILLIAMS, S,	4 Queens Avenue, Hinton, Essex, AT12 4MX	(01231) 346832

Text © 2007, Sue Taylor

Class 2 library catalogue

These books are in the blue box.
Please make sure you put them back in the right place
so that other children can find the books they want!

Allan **AHLBERG**	*Each Peach, Pear, Plum*
Jez **ALBOROUGH**	*Duck in the Truck*
Anthony **BROWNE**	*Willy the Wimp*
John **BURNINGHAM**	*Mr Gumpy's Outing*
Rod **CAMPBELL**	*Dear Zoo*
Eric **CARLE**	*The Very Hungry Caterpillar*
Lynley **DODD**	*Hairy Maclary from Donaldson's Dairy*
Julia **DONALDSON**	*The Gruffalo*
Eric **HILL**	*Where's Spot?*
Pat **HUTCHINS**	*Rosie's Walk*
David **MCKEE**	*Elmer*
Jill **MURPHY**	*Peace at Last*
Michael **ROSEN**	*We're Going on a Bear Hunt*
Maurice **SENDAK**	*Where the Wild Things Are*
Martin **WADDELL**	*Farmer Duck*

Text © 2007, Sue Taylor

Catalogue Index

TOYS

Action Toys	***631-641***
Art Materials	*496, 513, 516, **580-594***
Audio/CD/DVD	*528-529*
Baby and Early Years	*493-531*
Ball Games	*250-251, **602***
Bath Toys	*499, 513*
Batman	*632-634*

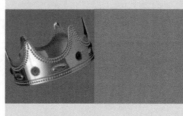  

Bob the Builder	*522*
Bratz	*568-656*
Cars and Trucks	*446-447, **616-629**, 639*
Construction	*512, 522-523, 630, **642-647***
Dolls/Accessories	***536-545**, 554, 557-575*
Dressing-Up	*535, 538, 558-559, 562-564, 630, 632, 635, 639-640*
Electronic Games	*435-438, 441, 535, 567, 573, 581, 630, 632-634, 638, 656-658, **660-671***
Electronic Learning Aids	*495, 500, **504-511**, 565*
Fashion Dolls	*562-575*
Fisher Price	*494-496, 504, 524-525*

Fimbles	*515*
Games, Boxed	*413, 449, 573, 630, **653-663***
Games Tables	*262-265, 441*
Go-Karts	***600-601**, 613*
Hot Wheels	*626-627*
Karaoke, Children's	*412, 528-529*
Kitchens (Toy)	*533-534*
Lego	*630, **642-644***

Text © 2007, Scholastic Ltd; photos in yellow panel: top left © Julie Elliot, top centre © Jeff Osborn, top right © Marja Flick-Buijs, middle left © Davide Guglielmo, middle centre and middle right © Jeff Osborn, bottom left © Barbara Bar, bottom centre © Jeff Osborn, bottom right © Andrzej Pobiendinski; photos in green panel: top left © Erke Tamiste, middle right © Jean Scheijen, middle left © Luis Rock, bottom right © Barb Ballard

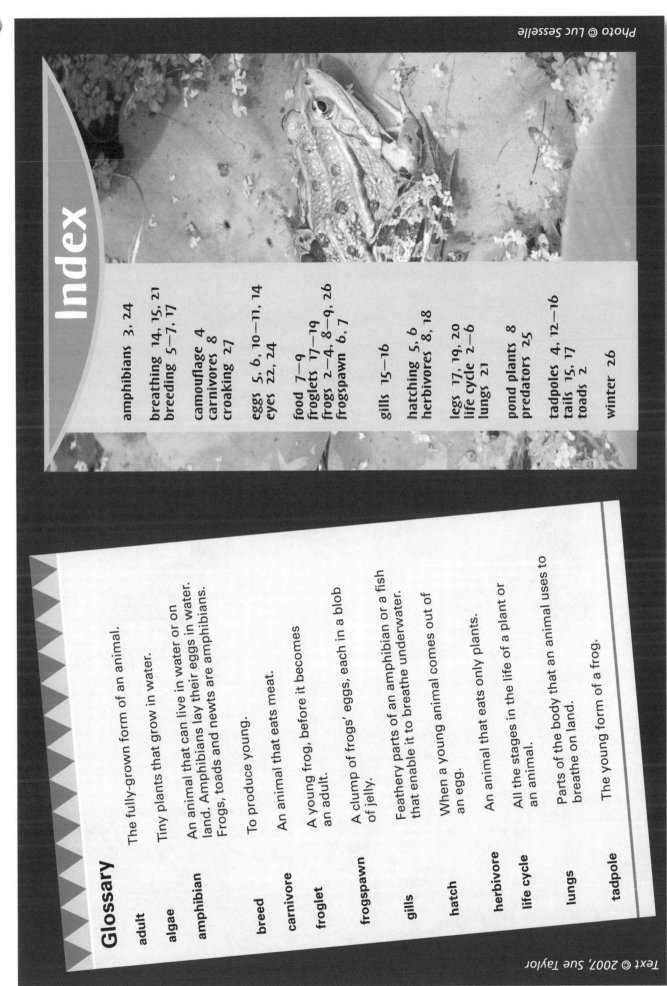

Photo © Luc Sesselle

Index

amphibians 3, 24

breathing 14, 15, 21
breeding 5–7, 17

camouflage 4
carnivores 8
croaking 27

eggs 5, 6, 10–11, 14
eyes 22, 24

food 7–9
froglets 17–19
frogs 2–4, 8–9, 26
frogspawn 6, 7

gills 15–16

hatching 5, 6
herbivores 8, 18

legs 17, 19, 20
life cycle 2–6
lungs 21

pond plants 8
predators 25

tadpoles 4, 12–16
tails 15, 17
toads 2

winter 26

Glossary

adult — The fully-grown form of an animal.

algae — Tiny plants that grow in water.

amphibian — An animal that can live in water or on land. Amphibians lay their eggs in water. Frogs, toads and newts are amphibians.

breed — To produce young.

carnivore — An animal that eats meat.

froglet — A young frog, before it becomes an adult.

frogspawn — A clump of frogs' eggs, each in a blob of jelly.

gills — Feathery parts of an amphibian or a fish that enable it to breathe underwater.

hatch — When a young animal comes out of an egg.

herbivore — An animal that eats only plants.

life cycle — All the stages in the life of a plant or an animal.

lungs — Parts of the body that an animal uses to breathe on land.

tadpole — The young form of a frog.

Text © 2007, Sue Taylor

The Life Cycle of a Frog

Adult frogs lay eggs in the spring. The eggs are called **frogspawn**. After a few days, the eggs begin to get longer and they develop small tails.

After about ten days, the eggs start to **hatch**. They are now called **tadpoles**. The tadpoles breathe underwater through **gills**. They eat **algae**.

When the tadpoles are about five weeks old, back legs start to grow. By the time they are ten weeks old, they have front legs as well.

When the tadpoles have their front legs, they come out of the water. Their gills have disappeared. The tadpoles have **lungs** inside their bodies for breathing. Their tails start to shrink. They are now called **froglets**.

The froglets start to feed on tiny animals such as flies and grow much bigger. They have become young frogs. The young frogs will live on land for two or three years. They then become adults and will return to a pond to **breed**.

Frogs are **amphibians**. They live some of the time on land but they lay eggs in water. Toads and newts are also amphibians.

Text © 2007, Sue Taylor; illustrations © Chris Rothero

Which comes first – the chicken or the egg?

A chicken is a bird. All birds lay eggs, usually in nests.
Nests may be in trees or on the ground.

The female chicken makes a nest on the ground and lays her eggs in it. She usually lays about ten eggs.

She sits on the eggs to keep them warm and protect them. Inside each egg the baby chicken begins to grow. It is called an embryo.

When the chick is ready to hatch, it uses a special tooth to break a hole in the shell. When the hole is big enough, the chick struggles out.

Baby chicks don't have proper feathers. They have a soft, fluffy coat called down. Feathers grow when the young chicken is a few weeks old.

When the chicken is about five months old, she is ready to lay eggs.

Text © 2007, Sue Taylor; photos: eggs © Miguel Ugalde, chickens on nest and chick with egg © Jozsef Szasz-Fabian, baby chick and chicken © Kate Childers

How does your garden grow?
The life of a bean

There are lots of different types of beans. There are broad beans, runner beans and French beans and many more. They all have pods with the bean inside. Peas also grow in the same way.

Seeds are usually planted in the spring. If you plant a bean in a glass jar with soil or blotting paper, you can watch it grow. Plants need water and light to grow. Put your jar on a sunny window sill and don't forget to water your bean!

If you plant your bean into the garden when it gets quite tall, you will able to pick the beans and eat them or grow some more plants!

First the bean grows roots. These go down towards the bottom of the jar.

Then it grows a shoot that grows up towards the top. It has two leaves at the end of the shoot.

More leaves grow as the plant gets taller. You should plant it in the garden now.

Now flowers grow on the stalk. Each flower makes a bean.

When the flowers die, the pods start to grow. The pods grow bigger and inside there are new bean seeds. You can eat these or save some and plant them next year to grow new plants.

Text © 2007, Sue Taylor; illustrations © Wai Yen Fu

Where does bread come from?

Bread is made from flour. Flour is made by grinding the **grain** (seeds) of plants called **cereals**. It is usually made from grains of wheat but it can also be made of oats, barley, rye or rice.

If the whole grain is used, the flour is brown and it makes **wholemeal** bread. If only the inside of the grain is used the flour is white.

In the past, people used to grow their own wheat, and ground flour to make bread by hand. Nowadays, farmers grow wheat in huge fields, and mills use machines to make flour. Modern bakeries use electric mixing machines and enormous ovens to make hundreds of loaves of bread. You can buy flour and make your own bread.

In the spring, the farmer **sows** the seeds.

During the summer, the seeds grow into tall plants. New seeds (grains) grow at the top of each plant stalk. In the autumn, the farmer uses a **combine harvester** to cut the crop.

The combine harvester separates the grain from the stalks. The stalks are left in the fields. This is called **straw**.

The grain goes to a flour **mill**. Here it is **ground** into a fine powder called flour.

The flour is put into bags and sent to the **bakery** to be made into bread (and cakes, buns and biscuits!).

The journey of a letter

Have you ever wondered how a letter or card gets to the person you have sent it to?

This is the story of the journey of a letter. Some letters travel just a short distance but others travel right across the world.

Mina Akhtar
44 Kent Road,
Hinton,
Essex,
AT12 3KU

Posting

When you send a letter or card to someone, you write their name and address on the envelope. Then you stick a stamp on the envelope and put it in the post box.

Collecting

A postman collects all the letters from the post box and takes them to the nearest sorting office.

Sorting

At the sorting office, the letters are put into different boxes according to where they are being sent.

Transporting

The mail is sent to the post office nearest to the address on the envelope. It might travel by van or train. If it is going abroad it may go by ship or by plane.

Sorting again

The letters are sorted again into bags for each postman or woman to deliver.

Delivery

The postman or woman puts the letter or card through the letter box of the right house.

Touch

Your skin can feel things that it touches.

Your body can tell whether something is...

...tickly... ...or scratchy.

...soft... ...or hard

...hot... ...or cold

Feeling things

Just inside your skin are lots of tiny touch receptors. They feel different things, and then send messages to your brain. They can feel...

...painful things ...tickly things ...hot things ...or cold things.

Oowwch! Giggle Phew it's hot! Brrrr!

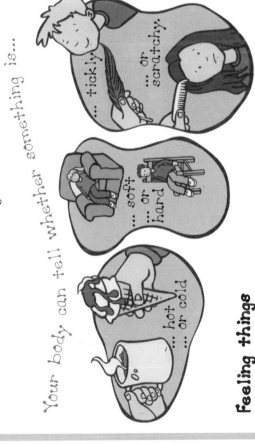

Oowwch! sting!

A bee has stung the girl's hand.

The touch receptors in her skin send messages along her nerves to her backbone.

Inside her backbone is something called her spinal cord.

The messages zoom up her spinal cord to her brain.

Her brain tells her that she has been hurt!

Spinal cord

Text extract and illustrations from "Usborne Flip-Flaps: How do your senses work?" by Judy Tatchell and Alastair Smith © 1997, Usborne Publishing Ltd

CHANGE

Ice, water, steam

Water is a liquid that can change when it gets colder or hotter.

When water freezes, it changes into ice. Ice is a solid.

When water boils, it changes into steam. Steam is a gas.

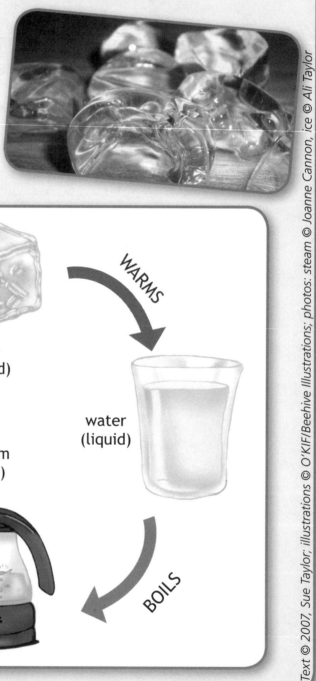

These changes are reversible.

Steam (gas) can change back into water (liquid) when it cools down.

Ice (solid) can change back into water (liquid) when it warms up.

Text © 2007, Sue Taylor; Illustrations © O'KIF/Beehive Illustrations; photos: steam © Joanne Cannon, ice © Ali Taylor

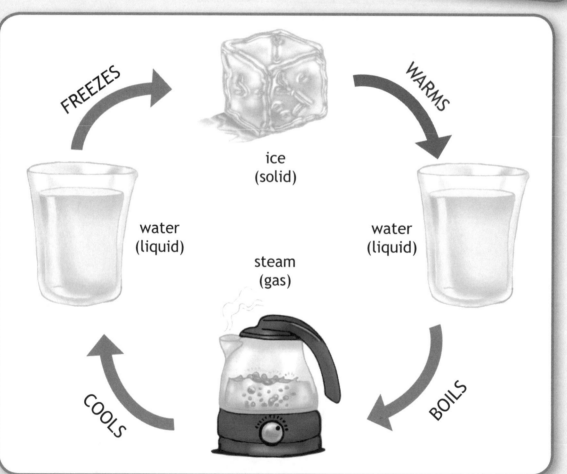

FREEZES

WARMS

ice
(solid)

water
(liquid)

water
(liquid)

steam
(gas)

COOLS

BOILS

Term 2: Explanations

Shuttle mission

In orbit

Doors open and satellite is launched

Doors close

Fuel tank falls away

Rockets fire

The Space Shuttle soars into the sky from its launch pad. The booster rockets and the external fuel tank fall away when they have used up all of their fuel.

In space, the astronauts launch a satellite with the help of the Orbiter's long robot arm.

At the end of the mission, the Orbiter's rocket engines fire to slow it down, and it begins to fall back to Earth. It glows with heat as it plunges back into the air around Earth. Then it glides down and lands on a runway like a plane.

Re-enters Earth's atmosphere

Booster rockets fall away

Glides back to Earth

Boosters parachute into the sea and are used again

Shuttle takes off

Text extract and illustration from "My Best Book of Spaceships" by Ian Graham © 1998, Kingfisher Publications plc

Extract 2

FIRE!

The Great Fire of London started on 2 September 1666, in Pudding Lane. Fires often happened in Tudor and Stuart times. Open fires were used for heating and cooking. Candles were used for lights. Accidents were likely with all these flames about. What was surprising about the Great Fire was how fast it spread, and how much of the city it burnt. Why was it such a bad fire?

To answer this question we have to look at the way that people fought fires at the time. We also need to look at how London was built. We are lucky to have the diary of Samuel Pepys, who was in London during the fire. He wrote down the things he saw and heard. This should give us some clues.

Text extract from "Our World: Tudor and Stuart Times" by Jane Shuter, Adam Hook and Judith Maguire © 1992, Jane Shuter, Adam Hook and Judith Maguire (1992, Heinemann Educational); photo © Csaba Polgar

Extract 1

A BAKERY BURNS DOWN

A year after the plague, London had a long, hot summer. The wooden buildings were as dry as firewood. It would only take a few sparks of fire to set a house alight.

Those sparks began in a bakery in Pudding Lane. The baker and his family and servants were asleep upstairs. In the bakery below, the dry wood kept to stoke the ovens caught fire. Soon flames were spreading through the building.

FIRE! FIRE!

The baker's family was awoken by neighbours and escaped from the fire by climbing across the roof to the next building. Everyone tried to put out the fire with buckets of water, but the fire was spreading faster and faster. By dawn, dozens of houses were on fire. A strong wind blew the flames from house to house, across the very narrow streets.

Text extract from "Beginning History: Plague and Fire" by Rhoda Nottridge © 1990, Wayland (Publishers) Limited

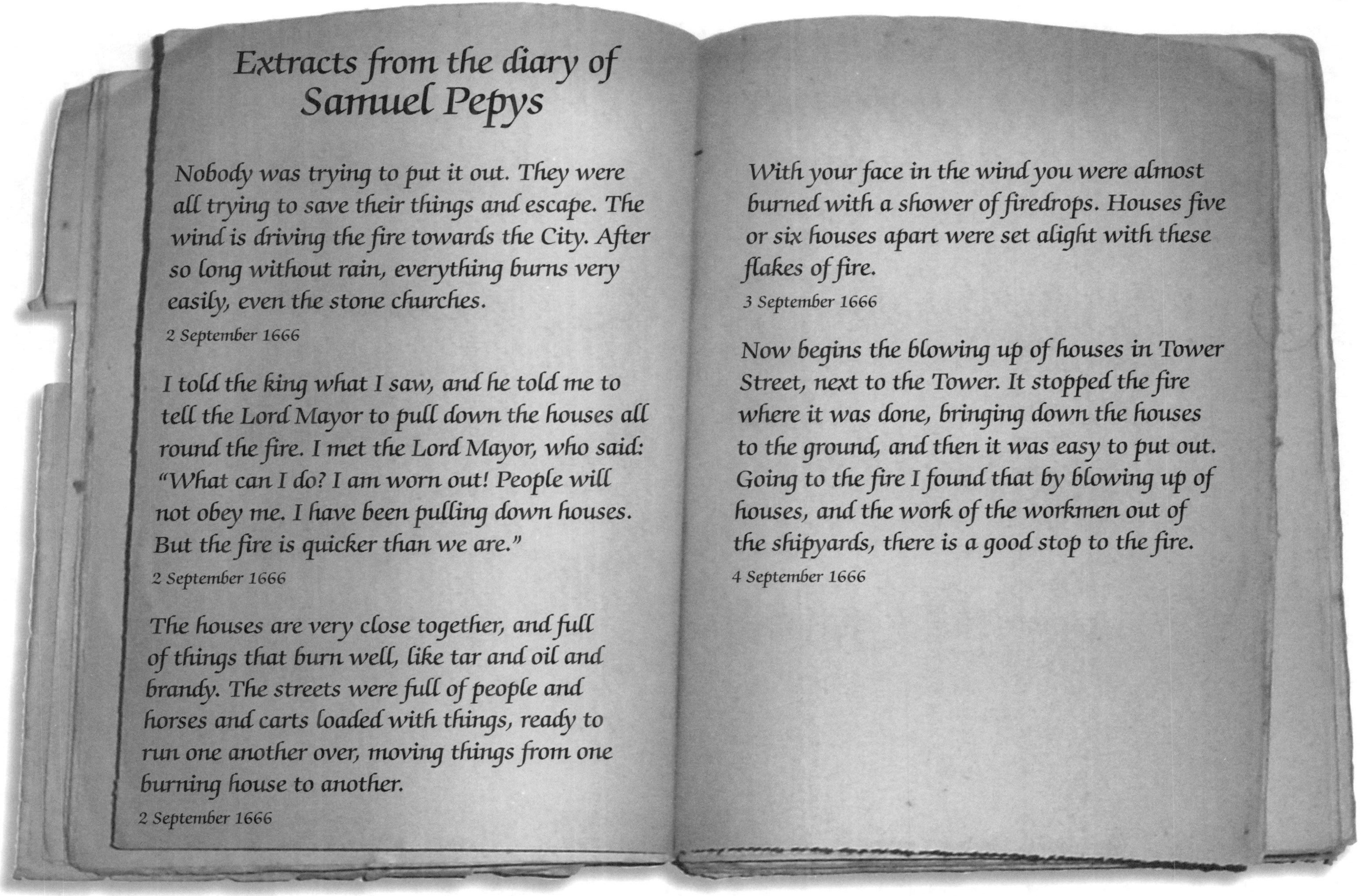

Extracts from the diary of Samuel Pepys

Nobody was trying to put it out. They were all trying to save their things and escape. The wind is driving the fire towards the City. After so long without rain, everything burns very easily, even the stone churches.

2 September 1666

I told the king what I saw, and he told me to tell the Lord Mayor to pull down the houses all round the fire. I met the Lord Mayor, who said: "What can I do? I am worn out! People will not obey me. I have been pulling down houses. But the fire is quicker than we are."

2 September 1666

The houses are very close together, and full of things that burn well, like tar and oil and brandy. The streets were full of people and horses and carts loaded with things, ready to run one another over, moving things from one burning house to another.

2 September 1666

With your face in the wind you were almost burned with a shower of firedrops. Houses five or six houses apart were set alight with these flakes of fire.

3 September 1666

Now begins the blowing up of houses in Tower Street, next to the Tower. It stopped the fire where it was done, bringing down the houses to the ground, and then it was easy to put out. Going to the fire I found that by blowing up of houses, and the work of the workmen out of the shipyards, there is a good stop to the fire.

4 September 1666

Text extract from "Our World: Tudor and Stuart Times" by Jane Shuter, Adam Hook and Judith Maguire © Jane Shuter, Adam Hook and Judith Maguire (1992, Heinemann Educational). Reprinted by permission of Harcourt Education.; photo © Jorge Vicente

NATURAL WORLD

 # ELEPHANT

Follow an elephant calf as it takes its first steps on its exciting journey through life in the African savannah.

Join the calf as it explores its surroundings, and watch it learn the skills it needs from the other members of the elephant herd.

•

Meet some of the other animals that share the elephants' watering hole.

•

Find out about the threats facing elephants in Africa and in Asia, and what can be done to protect these amazing creatures.

The author **Will Travers** has dedicated most of his life to wildlife and animal issues. He is co-founder and Chief Executive of the Born Free Foundation, a charitable organization that cares for wild animals. Its projects span five continents and include the rescue, conservation and protection of elephants, chimpanzees and big cats.

Other animals to meet in the **Natural World** series include:

CHIMPANZEE • GIANT PANDA • GREAT WHITE SHARK
KILLER WHALE • LION • POLAR BEAR • TIGER

ISBN 0-590-55825-0

£10.99   WAYLAND

9 780590 558259 >

Page from "Natural World – Elephant" by Will Travers © 1999, Wayland (Publishers) Ltd, by permission of Hodder and Stoughton Limited

Meet the elephant

Elephants are the largest land animals in the world. They are very strong, extremely intelligent and have remarkable memories.

Unlike most animals, elephants continue to grow throughout their lives – the older they get, the bigger and more impressive they are.

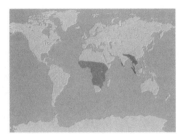

◀ Elephants live in many different habitats, including savannah, rainforests, swamps and mountains.

Key to map

African elephants

Asian elephants

There are two species of elephant. They are the Asian elephant (*Elephas maximus*) and the African elephant (*Loxodonta Africana*). They may look very similar, but there are important differences.

African elephants weigh between 4–7 tonnes, while Asian elephants weigh between 3–5 tonnes. At up to 4 metres high, the African elephant is also about a metre taller than the Asian elephant.

The tusks of an African elephant are bigger than those of the Asian elephant and its ears are also bigger. African elephants normally have rougher, more wrinkled skin than Asian elephants.

African elephant

Text extract, map and illustration from Natural World - Elephant by Will Travers, Text © 1999, Will Travers (1999, Wayland Publishers Ltd); Photo © Helen McGrath

REPTILES of long ago

From 260 million years ago until around 65 million years ago is known as the Age of Reptiles. During that time, reptiles were the most successful animals on Earth. Some kinds of reptiles that were alive then still exist today, such as crocodiles. Others, such as dinosaurs, died out suddenly. Nobody knows exactly why. We can find out about dinosaurs from their fossils.

There were many different kinds of dinosaurs. They were reptiles, like the lizards and snakes that are alive today.

ALL SHAPES...

Dinosaurs came in a wide variety of shapes. Some dinosaurs walked slowly on four legs. They had long necks and tails which they held out to help them balance. Others ran on two legs as ostriches do today. Some dinosaurs had bony plates and sails on their back to help them warm up and cool down. Many had vicious spikes, spines and horns on their bodies or heads to attack enemies with.

...AND SIZES

The biggest dinosaurs were the sauropods. They had long necks and tails and the largest were nearly 20 metres tall. They could weigh as much as sixty small cars. The smallest dinosaurs were tiny by comparison. Some were only the size of chickens.

DINOSAUR FOOD

Many dinosaurs ate plants. They had many tiny teeth designed for chewy food. They didn't need to move fast to catch their food. However, the smaller ones had to move fast to get away from meat-eating dinosaurs. The meat-eaters had fearsome, sharp teeth, perfect for tearing flesh. Some had terrible claws for slashing their prey.

Text © 2007, Scholastic Ltd; photo © Fotoredaction drs. online

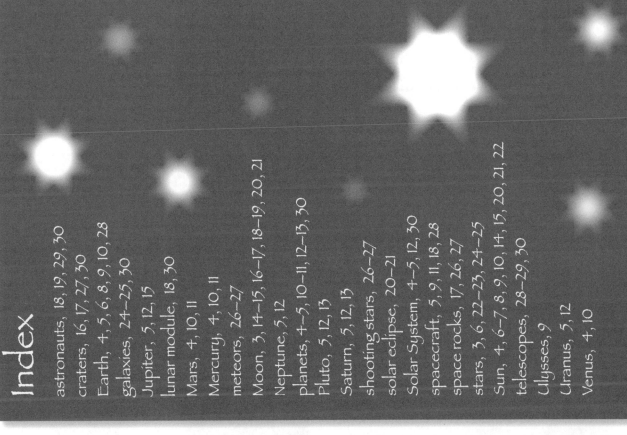

Index

Contents

Contents and index from "Usborne Beginners: Sun, Moon and Stars" by Stephanie Turnbull © 2003, Usborne Publishing Ltd; photo © Maciej Ciupa

What is the sun?

The Sun is a star. It is shining far out in
space, 150 million kilometres away.

The Sun is more than a million times bigger than the
Earth. It seems smaller because it is so far away.

The Sun looks brighter than other stars because
it is closer to the Earth than they are.

The Sun is billions of years old. The Sun that shone on
the dinosaurs is the same one that shines on us today.

The Sun's rays give us light and warmth. We call its light daylight.

We can only see the Sun during the day.
Everything on the Earth needs sunshine to live and to grow.

Sun fact
The Earth travels round
the Sun. It takes just
over one year to go
right round.

The Earth spins round once every 24 hours.

Text extract from "Sun and Us" by Jillian Powell © 1998, Belitha Press (1998, Anova Books);
photos: sun left © Lori Morris, sun right © Cheryl Empey, sun fact © Chris Watk

Day and night
We call the start of the day
sunrise and the end of the day **sunset**.

The Sun is often a lovely colour at these times.

Did you know the Sun is shining all
the time, even when you can't see it?

When we have night, the Sun is shining
on the other side of the world.

This is because the Earth is spinning
as it travels round the Sun.

On the side of the Earth facing the Sun it is daytime. On the
side facing away, the Earth is in darkness and it is night.

Sun fact
The light from the
Sun makes the
Moon shine.

Magnets

Magnets are objects which can attract certain other objects without touching them. Magnets come in different shapes. They can be curved, like horseshoes, or shaped like a bar, a ring or a cylinder. Magnets are used in lots of ways around the home. We can use magnets to stick notes to the fridge and to keep doors shut. They are sometimes used to link the carriages of toy trains and in other toys and games. Very powerful magnets are used to sort different materials for recycling.

Magnetic materials

Magnets only attract objects that contain certain materials, called magnetic materials. The metal iron is the most common magnetic material.

Magnetism

Magnetic materials are attracted to a magnet by a force called magnetism. This force can pass through some materials. A pin on a piece of paper will be attracted to a magnet on the other side of the paper. The magnet can make the pin move without touching it.

Magnetic poles

Every magnet has two poles at opposite parts or ends. These are called the north pole and the south pole. They are sometimes labelled N and S. The south pole may be painted blue and the north pole red. The north pole on one magnet will attract the south pole on another magnet. Two north poles or two south poles will repel each other.

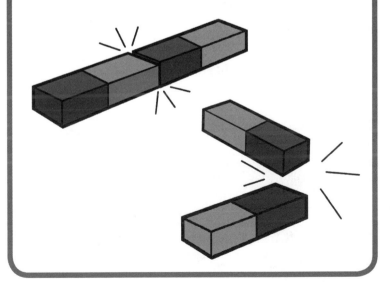

Text © 2007, Sue Taylor; illustrations © Theresa Tibbetts/Beehive Illustration

The Smith family in 2005

The Smiths have gone on holiday to Greece for two weeks. They like beaches and water sports.

Adam is six years old. He is learning to swim, using armbands. Megan is eight. She is playing on the beach. Their dad (Steve) is taking pictures of them with his digital camera.

Mum (Jenny) is calling to the children. She wants them to put on suntan lotion so they don't get burnt.

Today lots of people go abroad on holiday, to hot sunny beaches. They fly or take ferries to get there. While they are there they stay in hotels or apartments.

Text © 2007, Scholastic Ltd; Illustration © Jane Bottomley

The Watson family in 1905

The Watson family are at the seaside. They have gone there for the day.

Phyllis is six. She is learning to swim, using water wings. Her eight-year-old brother Arthur is building a sandcastle. Their mother (Mary) is sitting in the shade. Charles, their father, is reading.

People didn't need to worry about sunburn because they wore their ordinary clothes. If they needed more shade they used an umbrella.

Many people went to the beach for days out in summer. They went in the morning and came back in the evening. They travelled by train to get there.

Text © 2007, Scholastic Ltd; illustration © Jane Bottomley

The Seaside

Have you ever visited the seaside? What did you do there? Did you build sandcastles, explore rock pools, go for a swim?

The seaside is where the land meets the sea. It is a special place, with breaking waves, caves and sand dunes, seaweed, shellfish and sea birds.

Another name for the seaside is the coast. There are different kinds of coast all over the world. Some are rocky with few trees. Other coasts have long sandy beaches and palm trees.

What Lives on the Seashore?

Different areas of the shore have different types of wildlife. Sea birds gather on the wide, sandy beaches. Rocky parts of the shore may have lots of pools that are home to many animals.

What are Tides?

Did you know that the level of the sea rises and falls? This happens about twice every day. When the level of the sea rises it is called high tide, when it falls this is low tide.

At high tide, the beach is mostly covered by the sea. At low tide, the sea is sometimes far away and there is a large area of wet sand to play on.

As the tide goes out, seaweed, driftwood and other debris are often left in a line on the beach. This line is the high tide mark.

Text extract from "Step by Step Geography: Seas and Coasts" by Patience Coster © 1997, Patience Coster (1997, Franklin Watts); photos: background © Craig Jewell, seagull © Kevin Walsh, rocky coast © Andrzej Pobiendzinski

Contents

Contents

Contents

Text © 2007, Scholastic Ltd; photos: left © Natalie Souprounovich, centre © Mario A Magallanes Trejo, right © Tuco Egg

Email addresses

All email users have their own, unique email address. This ensures that messages are sent to the correct computers. Your ISP will either give you an address or allow you to choose one.

What does an address look like?

An email address has two main sections: the user name and the domain name. The two sections are separated by an @ symbol, which means "at". Here is a typical address:

mark@usborne.co.uk

user name   "at"   domain name

User name

The user name is often the name or nickname of the person who will receive the email. A name can be used in different ways. If, for example, your name was David Rowe, your user name could be: drowe, davidrowe, davidr, dave or David_Rowe (in the last example, the names are separated by a symbol called an underscore).

People whose email is sent to the same server have email addresses with the same domain name.

Domain name

A domain name is the name of the server to which the message will be sent. For home computer users, this is normally the name of your service provider's computer.

Part of the domain name is called the domain type. This tells you the kind of organisation where the server is located, such as 'gov' for a government organisation, and 'edu' or 'ac' for a school. Some domain types are listed below.

Domain names of computers outside the USA often end in a country code. For example, the code for the United Kingdom is "uk", France is "fr" and Australia is "au".

Dots (.) separate the various parts of the domain name.

Domain types

com or co	a commercial company
edu or ac	an educational establishment
gov	a government organization
net	Internet companies
org	organization

Each person can have an email address with their own user name.

Text extract and illustrations from "The Usborne Guide to e-mail" by Mark Wallace and Philippa Wingate; illustrated by Christyan Fox © 2000, Usborne Publishing Ltd

Spiders

Introduction

There are over 30,000 different species of spider, and they can be found all over the world. They are able to survive in hot and cold climates, in deserts, rainforests and grasslands. One can even live underwater. The only areas in which spiders are not found are the Arctic, the Antarctic and in deep oceans. All spiders are carnivores, but different species have different methods of catching their prey.

Arachnids

It is often thought that spiders are insects, but they are in fact a different kind of animal called an arachnid. There are significant differences between the two. Insects have six legs, whereas arachnids have eight. Typical insects are ants, bees, beetles and butterflies. Typical arachnids include spiders, scorpions and ticks.

All spiders:

have eight legs; have large jaws and sharp fangs to bite prey; have spinnerets that can spin silk for making webs.

Most spiders:

have eight eyes, but many cannot see very well; have hairs on their legs that can sense the movement of other animals nearby; have fangs through which they can inject poison into their prey;

Some spiders:

have six, four or two eyes; have no eyes at all – these are cave-dwelling spiders.

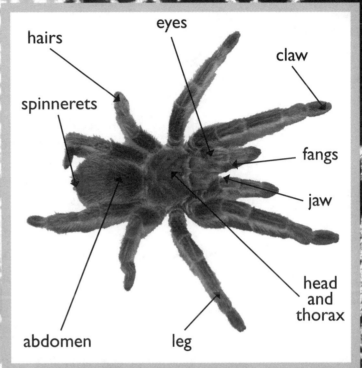

hairs · eyes · claw · spinnerets · fangs · jaw · head and thorax · abdomen · leg

	Insects	Arachnids
Legs	6	8
Antennae	2	none
Wings	most have 2 or 4	none
Has a poisonous bite or sting	some	nearly all
Eats plants	some	none
Eats other animals	some	all

Text extract from "Literacy World: Stage 4: Spiders and how they hunt" by Jason Amber © 1999, Reed Educational and Professional Publishing Ltd (1999, Heinemann Educational Publishers); photos: web © Valentina Frate, spider © Maarten Uilenbroek

Healthy food

Having a healthy, balanced diet means eating lots of different foods which give your body the nutrients it needs. Healthy foods include natural foods like wholemeal bread and wholegrain rice, beans and lentils. They contain lots of important nutrients like carbohydrates and vitamins but no added sugar, salt or additives. Organic food is food farmed without using chemicals.

Unhealthy foods are foods like sweets, lollies, cakes, biscuits and fizzy drinks. They contain lots of sugar, fat and additives and no important nutrients.
It is best to eat them as treats now and again.

▲ *Ice creams are eaten as treats now and again.*

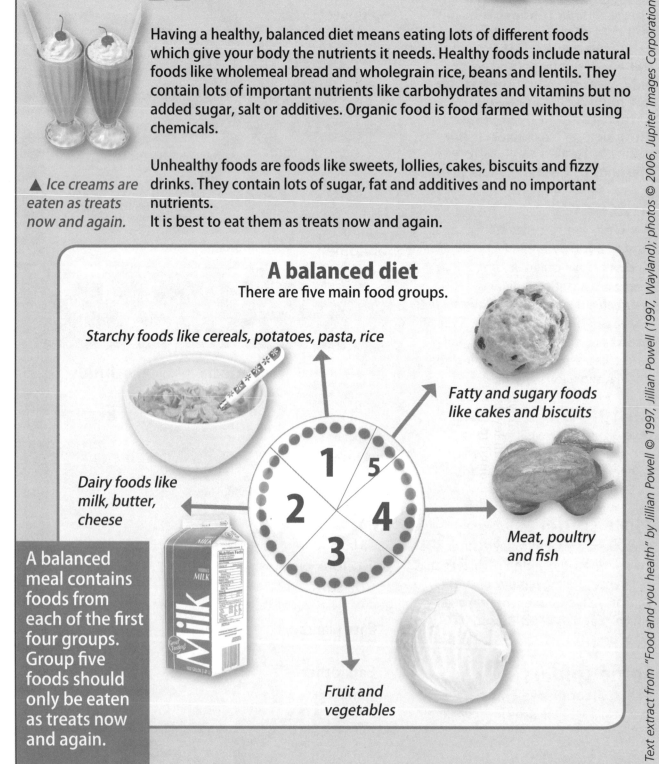

A balanced diet
There are five main food groups.

Starchy foods like cereals, potatoes, pasta, rice

Fatty and sugary foods like cakes and biscuits

Dairy foods like milk, butter, cheese

Meat, poultry and fish

Fruit and vegetables

A balanced meal contains foods from each of the first four groups. Group five foods should only be eaten as treats now and again.

MILK

Text extract from "Food and you health" by Jillian Powell © 1997, Jillian Powell (1997, Wayland); photos © 2006, Jupiter Images Corporation

WHY ARE RAINFORESTS IN DANGER?

Greenhouse effect

Every time we breathe, we give out a gas called carbon dioxide. The same gas is made in car engines and whenever we burn anything. It forms a layer round the Earth and traps heat, just like greenhouse glass. The heat warms the Earth and can cause droughts and other big changes in the world's weather. Trees use up carbon dioxide, so cutting down the rain forests is making this 'Greenhouse Effect' even worse.

Rainforests are among the most threatened places on Earth. Millions of trees are cut down each year for timber. Huge areas are also felled every day to make way for farming. Thousands of animals are probably becoming extinct every year because there is nowhere left for them to live. Even if new trees are planted, these places will never get their original wildlife back again.

Many kinds of beautiful forest birds and insects will never be seen again because their forest homes are being cut down. The problem is especially bad in South America and South-East Asia.

WHERE DO RAINFORESTS GROW?

Rainforests grow in places where there is lots of rain. Most rainforests are found in the tropics, on either side of the Equator. Most of the plants there are evergreen – they never drop all their leaves at once, but grow the whole year round in the hot, steamy atmosphere. Animals live at all levels in the forest, from the ground to the tree-tops.

Do you know?

Some rainforests are huge, but altogether they still only cover about one-twentieth of the Earth's surface. Even so, scientists believe that the rainforests contain more than half of the world's plant and animal species.

Text extracts and illustrations from Questions and Answers - Rainforest Animals by Michael Chinery, illustrated by David Holmes and Bernard Robinson © 1995, Kingfisher Publications plc.

Acknowledgements

The publishers gratefully acknowledge permission to reproduce the following copyright material:

Anova Books for the use of an extract 'What is the sun?' from *Sun and Us* by Jillian Powell © 1998, Belitha Press (1998, Anova Books). **Jill Bennett** for the use of 'Making dummy fireworks' from *Bright Ideas: Festivals* by Jill Bennett and Archie Millar © 1988, Jill Bennett (1988, Scholastic Ltd). **Harcourt Education** for the use of two extracts 'Fire' and 'Extracts from the diary of Samuel Pepys' from *Our World: Tudor and Stuart Times* by Jane Shuter, Adam Hook and Judith Maguire © 1992, Jane Shuter, Adam Hook and Judith Maguire (1992, Heinemann Educational); for the use of text extracts and images 'Puppets' from *Discovery World Stage F: Arts and Crafts Around the World* © 1997, Heinemann Educational (1997, Heinemann Educational); for the use of an extract 'ad-bl' from *Science Dictionary* © 1997, Reed Educational and Professional Publishing (1997, Reed Educational); for the use of 'Route map' text extract and illustration by Roger Fereday/ Linda Rogers Associates from *Discovery World Stage F: Maps* © 1997, Heinemann Educational (1997, Heinemann Educational). **HarperCollins Publishers Ltd** for the use of extracts 'Whale to which' from *Collins Junior Dictionary* compiled by Evelyn Goldsmith © 2000, HarperCollins Publishers Ltd (2000, HarperCollins Publishers Ltd). **Hodder and Stoughton Ltd** for the use of an extract 'Meet the elephant' and the title page from *Natural World - Elephant* by Will Travers © 1999, Will Travers (1999, Wayland Publishers Ltd); for the use of an extract 'A bakery burns down' from *Beginning History: Plague and Fire* by Rhoda Nottridge © 1990, Rhoda Nottridge (1990, Hodder and Stoughton); for the use of an extract from *Food and your Health* by Jillian Powell © 1997, Jillian Powell (1997, Wayland Publishers). **Kingfisher Publications plc** for the use of extracts and illustrations from *Questions and Answers - Rain Forest Animals* by Michael Chinery, illustrated by David Holmes and Bernard Robinson © 1995, Kingfisher Publications plc (1995, Kingfisher Publications plc) and for the use of extracts and illustrations 'Shuttle mission' from *My best book of spaceships* by Ian Graham © 1995, Kingfisher Publications plc (1995, Kingfisher Publications plc). **McGraw-Hill Book Company, Europe** for the use of text extracts from *Literacy World: Stage 4: Spiders and how they hunt* by Jason Amber © 1999, Reed Educational and Professional Publishing Ltd (1999, Heinemann Educational

Publishers). **Oxford University Press** for the use of an extract and illustration from *Oxford First Rhyming Dictionary* by John Foster © 2003, John Foster (2003, Oxford University Press) and an extract from *Oxford First Thesaurus* by Andrew Delahunty © 2002, Andrew Delahunty (2002, Oxford University Press). **Usborne Publishing Ltd** for the use of 'Easy pop-ups' text extract and an illustration from *The Usborne Book of Pop-ups* by Richard Dungworth and Ray Gibson © 1995, Usborne Publishing Ltd (1995, Usborne Publishing Ltd); for the use of 'Swedish hanging biscuits' text extract and illustrations from *You and your child: Christmas* by Ray Gibson © 1991, Usborne Publishing Ltd (1991, Usborne Publishing ltd); for the use of the extract 'Touch' and illustrations from *Usborne Flip-Flaps: How do your senses work* by Judy Tatchell and Alastair Smith © 1997, Usborne Publishing Ltd (1997, Usborne Publishing Ltd) and for the use of contents and index page from *Usborne Beginners: Sun, Moon and Stars* by Stephanie Turnbull © 2003, Usborne Publishing Ltd (2003, Usborne Publishing Ltd) and the extract and illustrations 'Email addresses' from *The Usborne guide to e-mail* by Mark Wallace and Philippa Wingate; illustrations by Christyan Fox © 2000, Usborne Publishing Ltd. **Valiant Technology** for the use of an extract 'Making sentences with Roamer' and an illustration from *The Roamer literacy pack* © 2005, Valiant Technology (2005, Valiant Technology) www.valiant-technology.com. **Watts Publishing Group** for the use of an extract 'The seaside' from *Step by Step Geography: Seas and Coasts* by Patience Coster © 1997, Patience Coster (1997, Franklin Watts).

Every effort has been made to trace copyright holders for the works reproduced in this book and the publishers apologise for any inadvertent omissions.